CHARLES D. DALY

AMERICAN FOOTBALL

By
CHARLES D. DALY
P. A., U. S. A.

With Many Diagrams by the Author
And Portraits of Prominent
Players and Coaches

Harper & Brothers Publishers
New York and London

CONTENTS

ILLUSTRATIONS

INTRODUCTION

THE author of this book desires to present a treatise on the game of football, primarily for the benefit of football coaches, football players, and the football public. The material is presented in a popular form, except in a few chapters where it has been necessary to limit the discussion to the technical side of the subject.

In general the author has tried to establish certain basic principles that govern the game and has laid down what may appear to be hard-and-fast rules for training and playing. But though he realizes that rules are largely a matter of individual opinion, he feels safe in saying that the principles which he has stated are sound as a result of their having been tried and proved during many years of successful application by some of the best coaches in the country.

Although the author treats his subject from the standpoint of the large college team with a squad of fifty or more men, and with

INTRODUCTION

one or two important contests at the end of the season toward which practically the entire effort of the team is directed, the principles and rules that apply on a large scale to the large-college team apply equally on a small scale to the little college, preparatory school, and even high school.

Therefore, the author hopes that *American Football* will serve as a reliable guide for all who want to know the principles of the game, but more particularly for the coaches and captains, upon whose knowledge of the game depends largely the success of their teams. The author desires to make grateful acknowledgment for certain material used in connection with this book to Colonel Graves, Colonel Thompson and Major Pritchard, U. S. A. He feels particularly indebted to Colonel Graves.

FOOTBALL AXIOMS

1. FOOTBALL IS A BATTLE. GO OUT TO FIGHT AND KEEP IT UP ALL THE AFTERNOON.
2. A MAN'S VALUE TO HIS TEAM VARIES INVERSELY AS HIS DISTANCE FROM THE BALL.
3. IF THE LINE GOES FORWARD THE TEAM WINS, IF THE LINE COMES BACKWARD THE TEAM LOSES.

GAME AXIOMS

1. MAKE AND PLAY FOR THE BREAKS. WHEN ONE COMES YOUR WAY, SCORE.
2. IF THE GAME OR A BREAK GOES AGAINST YOU, DON'T LIE DOWN: PUT ON MORE STEAM.
3. DON'T SAVE YOURSELF. GO THE LIMIT. THERE ARE GOOD MEN ON THE SIDE LINE, WHEN YOU ARE EXHAUSTED.

AMERICAN FOOTBALL

I

ORGANIZATION—CONDITION AND TRAINING

A REMARKABLE similarity exists between war and football. This is particularly manifest in their organization. In both war and football we have the staff and the troops. In both we have the supply department, medical branch, and the instruction branch. In both, the importance of leadership is paramount. The principles of war laid down by Clausevitz are the principles of the application of force. Just so in football, we have exactly analogous principles of the application of force and a similar organization.

There are five elements that enter into the organization of a football team: first, the material; second, the coach; third, the assistant coaches; fourth, the captain; fifth, the trainer and the doctor.

The Material

If the material at the start is to be without defect there must be the following:

1. Powerful and fast line material.
2. An experienced player available for quarterback.
3. Speedy, rugged, back-field men.
4. A reliable kicker who can get good distance.
5. Sure catchers for the back-field.
6. A back and a kicker, both of whom can pass.
7. Speedy ends who are sure tacklers and who can catch passes.

Unless the material has players capable of fulfilling these requisites, and good substitutes to take their place, the material is weak.

The above statement covers the ideal case. Ordinarily a coach is not fortunate enough to be blessed with such rounded-out material. If he is, victory will ordinarily perch upon his banner. In the ordinary case there are generally one or two weaknesses in the material which must be adjusted by skillful coaching.

It is the business of the coach to determine these weaknesses in both his own squad and in the enemy squad. His scheme of play

Two Successful Offensive Distributions

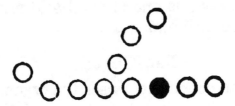

Normal attack developed into eight men on line of scrimmage
using direct pass.

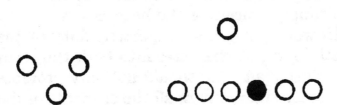

Concentration for a direct plunge with dispersion for passing.
A freak formation.

should then be so designed as to minimize his own weaknesses and still take advantage of those of the opponents. *Play to the other team's weakness* is one of the basic principles of both football and war.

The Coach

The head coach supervises the organization and its work. He takes charge of the first eleven when it assembles for dummy scrimmage or signals.

He is responsible for the organization, schedule, equipment, officials, and all other matters incident to the team's progress, not specifically in the hands of parts of the organization. The manager and his assistants are the supply officers of the head coach.

However, the most important duty of the coach is to put character into both the team and the squad. He should not only promote and secure harmony in all the elements of the organization, but at midseason, when "drive" and "fight" are the watchwords, it is the head coach who should secure that savage drive and desperate fight which are essential to victory.

Above all, the head coach is responsible for the spirit and morale of the team. He should so co-ordinate the effort of the parts of the organization that, as a result, there should be produced for the final contest a band of crusaders with nothing in their hearts but victory and with the unshakable determination to have that victory at all costs.

The Assistant Coaches

Five assistant coaches are necessary. Daily attendance from the first day's practice is imperative. More than seven assistants are bad. A large number of coaches produces an underdeveloped, characterless team. The coaches should be: one end coach, two line coaches, one back-field coach, one second-eleven coach. The position coaches make the team, by their work in position and group drill. The success of the team or its failure is mainly theirs.

The limit on the number of coaches prescribed above is not meant to rule out special coaches for particular performances. It is always advisable to secure a good instructor, if available, for work on the specialties, such as drop kicking, goal kicking, and passing.

Too much credit cannot be given to the position of assistant coaches for the success of the team. The individual excellence of each player arises from the work of the position coach. It is this individual excellence that spells victory, and the coach should have the credit for it.

THE CAPTAIN

A good captain accomplishes the following:

1. He plays his own position excellently in the final game. This is his first duty. All others are secondary.
2. He keeps the squad cheerful and in harmony with the coaches.
3. He advises the coaches of opinions or sentiments on the team at variance with their ideas.
4. He checks all decisions by the officials and claims his rights. He should know the rules thoroughly. Many slip-ups can happen due to the failure of the captain to secure his advantages under the rules. It is advisable, therefore, to detail another player who is well versed in and quick to appreciate the application of the rules to check the captain throughout a contest and to advise him, when necessary, of his rights. In other words, two heads are better than one.
5. He encourages the team in games when necessary. The captain should, however, be careful not to talk too much. A youngster chattering to his fellows all the time is an irritating influence, and a good captain should talk only when necessary and then in a manner which will appeal to his comrades.

Many captains have made the mistake of thinking that they were administrators instead of players. No more fatal error could be made. If the captain does nothing more than play his position well he is generally a success. If he attempts to do much else he is generally a failure. Quite often the worry of the captaincy requires the player to lay off considerably in order that he may be able to play his own position well. If he plays it exceedingly well, leadership will fall to him naturally. Nothing can make up for the failure of the captain to play his own position as well as his comrades are playing theirs.

The Trainer and the Doctor

The trainer and the doctor are responsible for the physical condition of the players. The doctor is directly responsible for all the injured. The trainer must see that the reserve energy of the players is never exhausted. He must also make sure that the prescribed treatment for injuries is carried out. He keeps the head coach informed as to the equipment of the players and supervises the fitting and use of pads and guards.

Mike Murphy, in an article on training a

football team, placed his finger on the crux of the matter. In substance, he said that players must be so trained that they will enter a contest eager to play and eager to make a touchdown. They must be, so to speak, tugging at the leash. Unless this strong desire to play and to win is present, there is something the matter with the physical or mental condition of the player.

CONDITION AND TRAINING

Organized practice each day rarely can consume more than two and one-half hours. There are ten weeks in the regular football season. Games are played on Saturdays, leaving five days per week for practice— that is, $5 \times 10 \times 2\frac{1}{2}$ hours, or 125 hours. Therefore, it is true that the preparation of a team for its final contest is a race against time.

The time of preparation is even more limited than stated above. Players over-train easily and often the regular practice must be shortened. From time to time it is, of course, necessary to withdraw certain players from practice in order to rest them. Physical condition is paramount. Coaching is secondary.

The following principles are standard in the training and development of a team:

1. Always underwork the players, individually and collectively.
2. Place no stress in the first half of the year on that character of fight which leads to the rapid exhaustion of nervous energy.
3. At midseason drive the team, individually and collectively, for at least one week. The fighting spirit here is paramount.
4. At least two and often three weeks from the final game, the team must be handled solely with the idea of perfecting what they already know and conserving their reserve vitality.
5. The result of good training is a mental attitude of eagerness for the entire afternoon's play, with muscles and sinew capable of sustaining the fight at high pressure.

Coaches always tend to overwork a player. They are inclined to drill a man (or a team) until the man draws on his reserve energy to sustain him. This is a great mistake. Drill should never draw on anything except the excess and ordinary energy of the player. The reserve energy must always be carefully guarded. It is used only in the final game. Its exhaustion at any other time results in overtraining. Recuperation takes not less than three weeks of almost entire rest. The guarding of the reserve energy of the individual players is the most important duty of the trainer.

The trainer should make a careful note of each player's physical and nervous qualities. He should keep a book showing the weights from day to day before or after practice, or both. He should carefully note the amount of work each man can stand without undue effort, the quickness of his recuperation, and the amount and kind of food he eats. Above all, it is his business to step in and advise the coach when a player should cease work. On this expert advice a good trainer defers to no one.

A good trainer keeps constantly in touch with the doctor who has charge of the injuries. He should seek his advice on matters of condition, as well as being entirely guided by him with respect to the injuries.

The doctor is responsible for the care and treatment of all injuries. In the caring for injuries the trainer works under his supervision.

Scrimmage should not be held if the doctor is absent. This rule is a vital one in safeguarding the best interests of the players and the sport.

Football injuries are characteristic. In

order to be competent to decide how soon certain injuries may be subjected to the strain of scrimmage, previous experience on the part of both doctor and trainer is necessary.

EQUIPMENT

All clothing and equipment should not weigh over eight pounds when dry.

Shoulder pads should cover the collar bone and be sprung over the point of the shoulder. They should be under the jersey.

Headguards should not be too large and should resemble a helmet rather than a cap.

A piece of light leather should re-enforce the jersey at the elbow joint.

The hands or wrists of line men should be taped.

The point and edge of each hip joint and the small of the back should be covered with a light felt pad about one half inch thick. This pad is sometimes re-enforced with leather.

The knee joint should be covered with a felt cover fastened below the knee or sewed into the trousers.

The thigh should be covered with a rigid guard sprung off the muscles of the leg.

Ankle supports should always be worn.

Shoes should be light in weight, close fitting, and flexible.

No player should be allowed to scrimmage who is not properly protected as stated above.

Whenever a man is injured, so that it is questionable as to his capacity to protect himself, due to being stunned, loss of speed, turning ability, or other causes, he should be instantly removed from the scrimmage. Always err on the conservative side.

Certain injuries are typical and characteristic of the game.

1. Tackle shoulder: Injury to the cartilage covering the point of the shoulder, due to a sharp blow. Player unable to raise elbow above shoulder. Not less than two weeks of absolute quiet for the shoulder required. When play is resumed a brace should be sprung over the injury, resting on chest and shoulder blade.
2. Bruised thigh muscle, "charley horse," "a poop." Will last, if properly treated, not longer than three weeks. Never massage. Bake, hot water, tape, and absolute rest.
3. Wrenched knee. Bake, hot water, and tape. A brace may be worn in practice. Where sinovitis may prove chronic, the player should give up football. Rest essential.
4. Blow on head. Recognized by small pupils of eyes, wabbly walk, or inability to multiply quickly. Should be removed from scrimmage

F. GORDON BROWN,
GUARD, YALE

E. H. COY,
FULLBACK, YALE

T. L. SHEVLIN,
END, YALE

instantly and turned over to doctor, and should
not play again that day.

5. Bruise on point or edge of hip bone. Hot appli-
cations, tape, and rest. Should not be trouble-
some, if properly treated, after two weeks.

6. Sprained ankle. Bake, hot water, tape, and absolute rest for very short while; then mild use.

The above remarks on ordinary football injuries are in no way meant to take the place
of the medical advice which should always be
present.

SCHEDULE

It is better to have too hard than too weak
a schedule. The teams played should demand the maximum effort without drawing
on the reserve energy. Fifty per cent of
them should be such that they could be held
in check by the substitutes. However, as
intimated, no more insidious element in development can exist than that of a weak
schedule.

It is well to play two teams unusually
strong on the forward pass.

Scouts should follow the work of all the
teams played that appear dangerous. Re-
ports should be submitted from the beginning
of the year.

The work of the team against an opponent with a strong kicking game should be carefully studied.

The last word on every item of condition and training is: *Never exhaust the reserve vitality of the players; always keep them eager for a whole afternoon's battle.*

II

FUNDAMENTALS

THE game of football is based on three
underlying fundamentals: tackling, interference, and following the ball. These are
called basic because the entire success of the
attack and defense depends on their skillful
execution by each and every man on the field.

INTERFERENCE

Advancing the ball by rushes is based on
the rule allowing interference in advance of
the runner. Offensive line work is really a
study in interference and is considered under
Position Play.

When the runner passes through the line
of scrimmage, or skirts it on a sweeping run,
or by any other means is running in the open,
open-field interference becomes of the highest
importance. This interference should be a
matter of drill.

There are several ways of interfering: No.

1 or 2 back, when covering the runner on a skin tackle play, may interfere and block the opposing end or halfback by advancing to him, and then, with wide steps and arms close to body, going forward and covering him. When the shock of contact is not great this may be called "covering interference." On an end run the backs often find it advisable to lunge with their shoulder at the opposing end or back, sometimes actually leaving the ground on a diving interference. This has the disadvantage of compelling the interferer to surrender control of his body. This may be called "diving interference." A skillful interferer often may jump at an opponent, sustaining the shock on his arms and still keeping his feet. This is a particularly effective form of open-field interference. This is "high interference." "Diving interference" is, of course, low. Another kind of open-field interference, which may at times be used on an end run, is where the interferer dives slightly to one side of the tackler and swings his legs across the legs of the tackler. This is effective for open-field work where the tackler is not close to the runner.

These various forms of interference should be drilled at least three days a week. The

basic nature of this work should be carefully
explained to the team. Although the matter
of drill is important, the player should have
it impressed upon him that, irrespective of

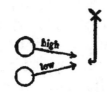

Two methods of attacking an end.

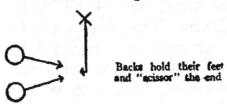

Backs hold their feet
and "scissor" the end

form or coaching, when it is his place to interfere, he must take the man out, skillfully
if possible—if not skillfully, by any other
method. The result must be obtained. The
tackler must be eliminated.

TACKLING

Good tackling is the result of daily trips
to the tackling dummy—Mondays excepted,
possibly. The men should be taught to
throw their body across the dummy, chest
against the thighs, head well beyond the off
2

leg, *eyes open*, arms and hands extended wide and gripping. Great stress should be laid in striking with the arms and holding on with the hands. A good handgrip is often the saving grace of a tackle. Good tackling is always low. However, if the situation is such that the tackler cannot get low or will not get the runner by going low, let him tackle any way he can. Knock him down with the shoulder, tackle him high with the hands or arms, but at all costs bring the runner down. The result must be obtained. The runner must be brought down.

The use of the hands and arms in getting by interference, in order to get at the runner, is almost a fundamental of good tackling. A good tackler is built with his hands and arms ready to extend in front of him and ready to strike his way by interference.

The judging of the speed of a runner is another essential of good tackling. The tackler should be paired off with another player and together they should drill in running down each other. All the practice of straight-arm work, change of pace, and dodging can be obtained in this drill by the runner. The tackler makes every movement except the actual lunge. The actual tackle should not be made. Actual tackling is best done at the dummy and in scrimmage.

FOLLOWING THE BALL

Following the ball is one of the attributes of all good players. Without it the best of teams will lose. With it, teams 50 per cent weaker will stand off their opponents. Eleven men following the ball every minute of the play means victory. It has been said that a man's value to his team varies inversely as his distance from the ball, and no saying was ever more true. Close following of the ball means that every man on the team follows the ball and never loses sight of it, whether his own team or that of the opponents has it. This is one of the keys to success in football.

Following the ball is best coached by harping on it throughout the season and making each individual player responsible on any long run, no matter whether the team be on the offense or defense. It may be drilled in a minor way by having two men practice passing on the run to one another, while two others attempt to intercept and spoil the pass. This passing drill is called "Passing and following the ball." It is possible that other drills may be devised.

The above are the essential fundamentals of the game of football. The minor fundamentals are:

1. All forms of kicking—punt, drop, placement, field goals.
   (a) Catching punts.
2. Carrying the ball.
3. Dodging.
4. Falling on the ball.
5. Charging by line men.
6. Use of hands by line men.

KICKING AND CATCHING

The various kinds of kicking and catching are so important that they are considered under a separate section. It need be said here only that all kinds of kicking and catching should be practiced a short time every day *before practice.* "Before practice" is specified because it is at that time that the attention of the players is keenest. After practice is undesirable because the player is liable to catch cold or to lessen his vitality for the week by too long practice.

CARRYING THE BALL

All the players should know how to "fix" the ball. It should be grasped between the wrist and the elbow, and held tight and close to the body. One point should be covered with the palm of the hand, the other point with the crook of the elbow. Players should be cautioned against swinging the arm and carrying the ball loosely. When running, the ball should never be changed, on ordinary plays, from one arm to the other. At times an old, skillful player can slip the ball from one arm to the other when running free in the open, but this is a practice which should be discouraged. The ball, on wide slants and wide runs, should be carried in the arm farthest from the scrimmage line, thus permitting the free use of the arm nearest the opponent. On close slants and plunges, the ball should be placed by the quarter firmly on the belly of the back receiving it. One of the back's hands should cover the upper part of the ball, the other the lower half, with the quarter's hand in between. The long axis of the ball should be parallel with the ground.

Receiving and fixing the ball is an essential drill of back-field work and a matter that must be watched the entire season. It is the answer to all the fumbling in scrimmage work. Some backs will be found, at times, who seem to be unable to receive or fix the ball and hit the line at the same time. Such backs are natural fumblers and are not available material.

It should be stated that a back hitting the line should not hurry to fix the ball at the

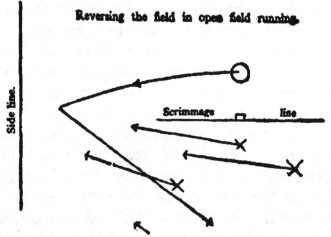

Reversing the field in open field running.

expense of his effort to go forward. He may and should carry it covered with both forearms until the opportunity for fixing it is at hand.

DODGING

All the members of the team should practice dodging in the early season. The converse is also true—that is, that the entire squad should practice pocketing a dodging runner and negotiating his straight arm.

The backs should practice a few dodges every day. This work should be of two kinds: close dodging and open-field work where the back "reverses the field." Close dodging may be practiced by making the backs in turn run in and out among a line of their fellows or by setting one man with the ball to dodging around among three tacklers close to him. Reversing the field consists in making the tacklers run full speed toward the runner, who watches his opportunity and by a sharp change of direction drives through a space in the oncoming field of tacklers, who must reverse their direction to cross again the path of the runner. The best open-field runners have used this method considerably. It consists in running for the open on a straight line at full speed and then sharply reversing the field by cutting directly across the line of oncoming tacklers. Often the back, after crossing the line of tacklers, will find himself in the open field with nobody near him. This idea should be carefully explained to the backs and it should be practiced as best it may be.

FALLING ON BALL

Falling on the ball is dangerous and should be practiced with great care and only at intervals. Line men should never be required to run after the ball and throw their bodies on it. The result of such work has always been injurious to shoulder, elbow, hip, and knee. There is very little advantage to line men in falling on the ball. When they do practice it, the ball should be placed five or six feet in front of them or rolled gently along the ground on its side. The line men, as also the backs, should be cautioned not to injure themselves, and nobody with an injury should be allowed to fall on the ball. Backs should fall on the ball gently about three days a week in the beginning of the year to harden themselves by the shock of hitting the ground. In midseason this work should be reduced, but not altogether eliminated.

The player falling on the ball should throw and drop his body in front of and across its path, surrounding the ball with his arms and legs. He should not attempt to roll over and come up on his feet.

The last word on falling on the ball is that it is dangerous work and should command the care and watchfulness of the head coach.

CHARGING BY LINE MEN

Although an instantaneous start is not all-important to a back, it is all-important to a line man, particularly offensive line men. The ability of an offensive line man to start sharply and powerfully from a strong stance to a hard charge, which is properly followed up by his feet with short steps, marks the critical point of the rushing attack.

If the team has a starting signal, the charge and the signal should be practiced constantly for the various plays, against a dummy defense. If the team starts with the ball, the drill becomes even more important.

A detailed discussion of this, and charging, is made under Position Play. It will suffice to say here that the offensive line should be practiced daily in getting off with the ball or the signal in order to get the jump on their opponents. It is the key to the success of the rushing attack, and too much time or care cannot be spent on it. Every detail of the stance of the player should be given the most careful consideration.

The positions of the feet, arms, elbows, and hands require careful study in each individual case. Slight modifications of stance for different players are often necessary. But the result should be the same, so far as getting the jump on the opponents and carrying through the charge is concerned.

This point should be made in regard to line position. The weight of the player should be carried on his legs. A hand may sometimes be used with which to balance the body, but it is of the highest importance that the line man play the game on his legs.

Line play is a combination of fighting and wrestling. The position of a wrestler about to begin a bout is almost identical with the stance of a line man, except that it is higher. The position of a fighter mixing it up in close work with his opponent is also almost identical in its elementals with the position of a line man carrying through his charge. The wrestling mat and the fighting ring have been the source of the best information on line play. It will pay line men to study both.

Use of Hands by Line Men

The key of good defence work is aggressive breaking through by the line men, which depends for its success on the use of the hands.

The general theory of retaining control of one's body and holding the weight in hand should be carefully explained to the entire team. The success of this principle in defensive line work depends on the sharp, aggressive use of hands.

The principle of retaining control of one's body or weight is that a player either in tackling, interfering, charging, or breaking through should not commit himself until he is sure of doing effective work. Once committed to diving interference, or once having allowed the opponent to get under the arms close to the body, it may be said that the player has passed control of his body or weight to the opponent, to be steered as the opponent may desire. This is a wide principle in all athletics and is no better exemplified in boxing or wrestling than in the game of football. Keep your weight in hand, under control.

Keeping opponents away from the body when the play is directed at the defensive player is dependent upon the sharp, aggressive use of hands. Breaking through by spreading the offensive line or by slicing through is also dependent upon the use of hands. The answer to hard, sharp charging is the harder and sharper use of hands by the defense.

It is to be noted that the rules of the game of football practically state that the offen-

sive line men must stand on the line of scrimmage with their heads protruding for the
defensive players to use their hands on.
Drills in hitting-power and striking the head
are essential to the most effective line work.
Guarding the head, of course, becomes essential to the offensive line, but this, in the heat
of scrimmage, is often ineffective. It is true
that, even with long and careful drilling, defensive line men are able to hit a line man
on the head only occasionally. If one
investigates the statistics, he will find that
out of one hundred attempts only about
thirty are successful.

Powerful striking of the opponent on some
part of his body is essential to the best defensive line work, and it should be drilled
constantly. The hands should at times be
kept absolutely quiet. At times the arms
should be swung back and forth. The
charge should always be accompanied with
hard striking with the arms or hands. It is
the secret of good defense.

Charging and the use of hands should be
an important part of the group-work practice
each day. The line coaches should put two
lines opposite each other (never more than
fourteen players, all told), and then they

should go into every detail of this work, which is so essential to good position play.

SUMMARY

A team skilled individually in these fundamentals is bound to be strong. A team without this individual skill is bound to be weak. The excellence of the team is limited absolutely by the excellence of the individual players. The excellence of the individual is measured by his skill in executing the above fundamentals.

III

THE OFFENSE

FOOTBALL is a war game. The most remarkable similarity exists between the basic principles of combat in war and in football. The War Department has published a book known as the *Field Service Regulations* for the government of troops in the field. One chapter of this book is devoted to combat operations and in its beginning are enumerated the great underlying principles of combat in football.

Let us make these changes and quote. In doing so we are stating the great principles of both war and football.

COMBAT

Combat is divided into two general classes—the offensive and the defensive. The defensive is divided into the purely passive defense and the temporary defense, which has for its object the assumption of the offensive at the first favorable opportunity.

Decisive results are obtained only by the offensive.

Aggressiveness wins battles. The purely passive defense is adopted only when the mission can be fully accomplished by this method of warfare. In all other cases, if a force be obliged by uncontrollable circumstances to adopt the defensive, it must be considered as a temporary expedient, and a change to the offensive with all or part of the forces will be made as soon as conditions warrant such change.

COMBAT PRINCIPLES

1. Individual superiority insures success.
2. Unity of command is essential to success.
3. Simple and direct plans and methods are productive of the best results in war and football.
4. Avoid dispersion; concentrate for action.
5. Some reserves are essential.
6. The flanks in an action must be protected.
7. Reconnaissance continues throughout the action,

1. Individual superiority in football is directly analogous to fire superiority in war and it means success. It is not plays that win football games; it is the development of the individual excellence of the players to the point where individual superiority in combat is secured.

2. Divided leadership on or off the field of combat spells defeat in football as well as in war. There are few colleges that cannot recall disastrous years due to the violation of this principle.

3–4. Of all the great causes of defeat, the greatest arises from violating the rule of simplicity. Under the great stress of combat only that which is simple, clear, and capable of execution by the player of ordinary ability can be consummated with success. Allied with this rule of simplicity is the principle which states that dispersion in combat spells defeat. Complexity and dispersion go hand in hand as the Charybdis and Scylla to which 80 per cent of all defeats are due.

6–7. It is well understood that a play unprotected on the flank cannot succeed, and there is no need to point out to the coaching systems that maintain telephone communications with observers during games that "reconnaissance continues throughout the action."

These great principles of combat in war are the great principles of combat in football and they are violated by those doing so at their peril.

The Attack

The attack in football may be by rushing, by kicking, by passing, by deception, or by a combination of any two. A good team is skilled in all methods of attack. Generalship and the attack are so closely allied that the one cannot be appreciated without an understanding of the other. Scores resulting from a well-directed, effective attack are the object of the attack.

BY RUSHING

Various distributions of the eleven on the attack are permissible. The following standard distributions are in general use:

Seven men on the line of scrimmage, with the ball and center in the middle of the line; seven men with an unbalanced line of four men on one side of the center and two on the other; eight men on the line of scrimmage, with five on one side of the ball and two on the other; eight men, with four on one side and three on the other. The back-field unit in general arranges itself behind the middle of the offensive line, distributed either in tandem or parallel to the rush line at a distance that will permit the unit to hit the line as quickly as possible, going at maximum speed.

Concentration is the keynote of the distribution for a successful attack. The position of the ball with respect to the distribution is of no consequence, provided that it is placed along the line of scrimmage so that the runner is not delayed on any drive or slant.

3

Destruction or sweeping aside of the opposing force is the method of advance.

All concentrations have the same lines of

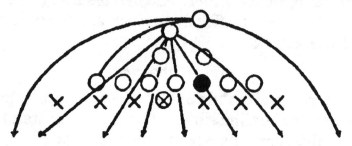

Lines of attack on the offense.   From behind the concentration
the backs, or "shock troops," may assault any interval or the
support of any interval in the opposing line of defense.

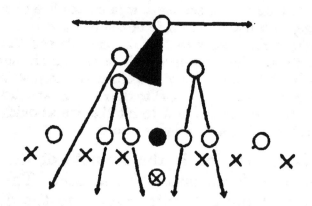

Lines of attack from the kick formation.   The vital area
when kicking is shaded.   This space must be protected at all
costs.

advance, irrespective of the position of the
ball.   There are two straight drives through

the middle of the line, two close slants inside
the defensive tackles, two wide slants outside the defensive tackles, and two runs
around the ends.

This gives eight plays in the running
attack, and there can be no more or no less.
The end run and the wide slant to the short
side are weak.

The following principles are basic in the
attack:

1. The line must advance. If it cannot remove the
   resistance it must get out of the way itself.
2. The backs must start immediately and hit the
   line at full speed.
3. Delay of any character is fatal.
4. Sending men away from the attack for deception
   weakens the attack.
5. If the runner takes more than five steps behind
   the line of scrimmage the play is weak.
6. If the ball is behind the line of scrimmage for any
   reason such as line divides, splits, crisscrosses,
   or brain storms, for more than the time it takes
   a fast man to start and to take five steps running
   (say, one and one half seconds), the play is
   weak.
7. If the line advances, the backs should go through
   to the secondary defense. At least once out of
   three times they should pass the first secondary.
8. Forwards and interference, irrespective of other
   duties, always guard the line of the play until
   the runner has passed.

9. Forwards more than twice removed always go through ahead to the secondary.

This statement of the principles of the running attack is, of course, general. Any distribution that gives proper concentration is good. The backs may be arranged in any way. The ball may be in any position along the line of scrimmage. Any concentration, however, must advance on the lines stated. Having complied with these underlying principles, the issue becomes one of individual excellence.

LINE PLAY

In general, the seven men on the line of scrimmage play foot and knee together, shoulders and feet square, weight over legs, a little weight on one hand. In general, the men at the point of attack drive straight forward and carry their opponents back. Those once removed charge close to those at the apex. The apex men "pass their opponents along" to those once removed and go through on to the secondary. Diving opponents must be steered aside, stepped over, or brought up. There is nothing that can overcome the failure of the line to charge in front of the play. Failure in the charge is ruination to the attack. *If the line goes forward the attack advances and the team wins. If the line comes backward the team loses.*

Seven Normal Offensive Distributions

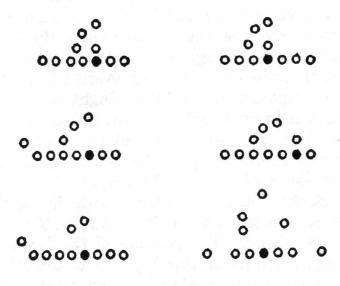

These seven diagrams show the normal offensive formations. It will be noted that simplicity and concentration are paramount. The position of the ball varies. These formations are of the kind used by practically all successful teams.

Success in this feature is paramount even when the attack lacks scoring strength, as it makes the defense concentrate against it.

No detail or study is too trivial or exacting in perfecting the offensive line.

OFFENSIVE BACKS

The offensive backs are the striking unit. They may not directly help one another, but the concentrated shock of their rush will often drive the line forward when the issue of the charge hangs in the balance. Starting which causes the back to overreach on his first steps is to be avoided. Slight loss at the start is insignificant as compared to hitting the line with maximum effort. Gathering power culminating in the shock of hitting the line is what should be sought.

Backs crouch in a position with the weight three quarters on the legs and one quarter on one hand. The position of the feet and weight admits of starting in any direction. The backs in front of the ball must be trained in helping the line on drives and close slants.

Herewith is outlined a plan of a simple direct assault on the opposing defense. The formation assumed is the classic distribution with four men on one side of the center, the long side, and two men on the short side. The back field is arranged behind the middle of the offensive line in tandem. The backs are referred to as Nos. 1, 2, and 3, in the order of their position from the line. That is, the man at the head of the tandem who is nearest the line is called No. 1.

STRAIGHT DRIVES—BUCKING THE CENTER

In these two plays the four men in front of the play advance together—the apex men going through on the secondary defense

Standard Plays in Execution

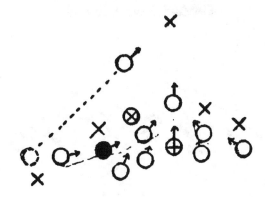

The Play Straight Ahead

This diagram shows the wedging rushline with linemen and end through in front of the runner.

after passing their opponent along. The long side end goes through to the secondary. No. 1 back goes through in front of runner if the charge is successful. If not, he works to the outside. No. 3 back strikes the line in rear of the quarterback. The No. 2, or middle, back strikes the line with the ball going through, as signaled, on either side of the middle line man.

CLOSE SLANTS—CROSS BUCK TO EITHER SIDE

In these two plays, all the offensive line in front of the play, except the end, work to turn the guard in. The end checks the tackle

Standard Plays in Execution

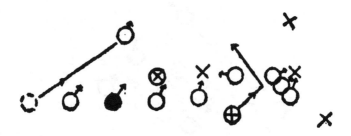

A Close Slant

until the two backs in front of the ball arrive and crash into him. This is the strongest play in football. On the goal line, this slant noses out around the tackle and No. 2 back takes the end. In any territory the No. 2 back is responsible for an in-driving end.

No. 3 carries the ball. After passing through the line he turns and "reverses the field." The removed end, after protecting the line of the play until the runner is well started, goes through to the secondary.

WIDE SLANTS—OFF-TACKLE PLAYS

In these two plays the offensive rush line pins the opposing end of the defensive rush line in place and the play then "skins" by

Standard Plays in Execution

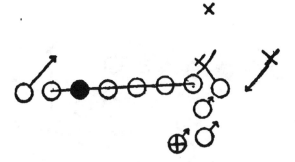

The Off-Tackle Play

"off tackle." No. 1 back boxes the tackle if the end has failed to do it. If the tackle is boxed, No. 1 goes on to the defensive back. No. 2 takes the end. This play is executed on a slight swing, not on a straight line as with drives and close slants. No. 3 swings out or reverses the field, at his option. The removed end and tackle go through to the secondary, after protecting the line of the play.

End Runs

These plays start parallel to the rush line. If the end comes well across, Nos. 1 and 2 hold him out, the runner swinging in and

Standard Plays in Execution

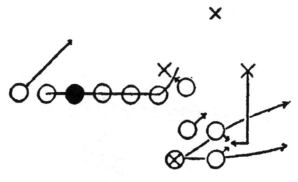

The End Run

then out. If the end drives in, No. 2 takes him, the runner goes outside, No. 1 and the quarterback cut inside the end, and meet the runner outside. The principles of open-field running then apply.

The method of play outlined above is that

in which a wedge is driven through the defense on the straight drives. On the close slants a hole is opened by driving the defensive guard in and the defensive tackle out. On the wide slants and end runs the defensive tackle is pinned in place and skirted. Simple, clean-cut, fast, direct assault is the keynote.

There is another method of line play used by some teams when the direct pass is used.

Standard Plays in Execution

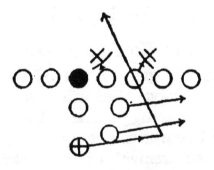

A Reverse Play

The direct pass permits of an eighth man permanently on the end of the line of scrimmage. It is the practice of some coaches to pair off these eight men against four of the defensive line men, neglecting the defensive line man farthest removed. In this method, sometimes one defensive line man is carried back and sometimes another. This is taken advantage of by developing a style of play where the backs, after having started, run at medium speed parallel to the rush line and then drive by the tackle by making a right-angle turn when opposite him. If the tackle blocks the play, the runner noses back toward the center and tries to work through, where either the defensive guard or center has been carried back. The usual drives, slants, and end runs are also used with all the essential elements of the simple direct assault.

The Kicking Attack

The kicking game is an offensive rather than a defensive measure. A good kick transfers the struggle one third the length of the field nearer the opponent's goal. The essential requirement of the distribution is that it shall thoroughly protect the kicker. It is the strongest forward-pass formation.

The general formation is with three line men on either side of the ball. The kicker should be eight to ten yards directly behind the middle of the line, with two backs in front of him on the side of his kicking foot, so placed that they can protect the vital space in which the ball rises from the kicker's foot. The fourth back protects the kicker on the side away from his kicking foot.

Running plays are executed on the same principles as in the close attack. Some schemes of offense have even moved the defending backs close to the line and distributed the line men as in the running attack. There is this difference in the play of the line, however: the line is free on all drives or slants to open holes and allow the runner to go through free. On sweeping runs, which have recently been somewhat effective, owing to poor defensive end work, the line men protect the line of the play, the removed side swinging back into the interference.

The essential feature of the open formation is the kick. The essential feature of the kick is distance, with sufficient height to enable the ends to cover. The kick should advance the ball at least thirty yards beyond the line of scrimmage.

PROTECTION

In order to protect the kick, the line holds fast. Nobody goes down with the ball except the ends. The line does not charge. It sustains the opponent's charge and holds fast from tackle to tackle. In doing this the individual members of the line are careful not to allow the opponents either to spread them or to jump over them.

The line men are free to go down the field after they hear the ball kicked. The removed tackle may go slightly before the kick, provided he is sure that in leaving his position he does not jeopardize the kick defense. Good coaching will enable linemen to time their start and the kick very closely. It is always safest to wait for the kick. The kick should take not more than two seconds against a strong opponent.

The defensive backs form protection on both sides of the kicker. The back on the side away from the kicker's foot, usually the quarterback, if attacked by two men, takes position well back and moves forward at that fraction of a second when the opposing line man starts to cut through in front of him. The situation is handled similarly if the back is attacked by three men. If only one man comes through, the back may handle him from his position under the line or back of it. Sometimes a quarterback can handle two men from his position under the line by driving the inside man out against his partner.

The defensive backs on the side of the kicker's foot form an arc behind which the ball is kicked. They sustain the charge and are careful neither to spread nor to allow opponents to jump over them. Their work is vital and they must never fail.

The kicker is responsible for his protection being in the right position. He must also see to it that he and his protection take plenty of distance. The answer to aggressive charging is "more distance" or a "fake kick" at the fast opponent, or both.

The kicker must kick behind his protection. Kicking, like catching, is inherent in the individual. Rarely do two men kick exactly alike. Rarely are kickers "made."

THE ENDS

When the ball is put in play for a kick, the ends are called upon to cover it—the most important duty of their position. They start from an unobstructed position, dig like a sprinter for fifteen yards, note the direction of the kick, and swing down upon the catcher from the outside. Generally they slow up at the end of their run so as not to overrun the catcher. A good end at times takes a chance and lands the catcher going full speed. But when the ends slow up, they must be careful to watch out for the opposing ends or halfbacks interfering from the rear. If they encounter obstruction while starting or running, they use their hands and arms without diminishing their speed.

THE LINE DOWN THE FIELD

The line men drive down the field, spreading out like a fan, and altering their direction

Standard Deceptions

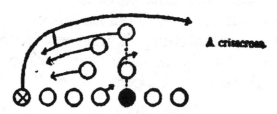

A crisscross.

according to any movement the catcher makes. Of course, the backs follow the line.

These principles are basic in the kicking attack.

1. The kicker must get his kick off within two seconds.
2. The kick must go at least thirty yards and be high enough to be covered.
3. The line and defensive backs must hold.

4. The kicker must kick behind his protection.
5. The ends must tackle the catcher with little or no run back.
6. The defense must hold the attack of the opponents and the back field catch the return kick. The issue is then one of individual excellence.

THE DROP KICK

When the attack by running, passing, or kicking finds itself in the vicinity of the opponent's goal and elects to try a field goal, a regular-kick formation is taken.

The only difference between the drop-kick formation and the regular-kick formation, in both distribution and duties, lies in the ends.

The ends in the drop-kick formation play in close and block until the kick is made. They then resume their down-field duties.

In all drop-kick formations, all the backs, especially the kicker, are safety men—that is, they recover a blocked kick.

All runs and passes may be executed from drop-kick situations. Indeed, the drop-kick formation near the opponent's goal, threatening run, kick, or pass, is one of the quarterback's strongest weapons.

The final word on the kicking game is that it is an offensive weapon. Those teams that resort to it only when compelled to do so

4

and after their rushing or passing attack is stopped make a great mistake. Quarterbacks, before they leave the kindergarten of football, must learn to "press the kicking

Standard Deceptions

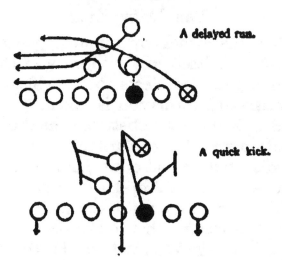

A delayed run.

A quick kick.

game." The successful quarterback must know its principles thoroughly. Most closely contested games are kicking contests, from which the break and the opportunity are developed.

THE ATTACK BY FORWARD PASSING

The forward pass is executed from any formation. It is always made to an open space and almost always received on the run.

CHARLES BRICKLEY, FULLBACK, HARVARD

For both offense and defense the question is one of the receiver getting to an open space uncovered. These open spaces exist in the center territory between the wing backs or to the outside flanks of the wing backs. Open territory exists in rear of all the defensive backs. It also exists close to the line of scrimmage in rear of the charging end and tackle. Open spaces can be made by deception. For instance, both ends, by leading out into the open, may draw the wing backs away from their territory. A halfback may then receive in the vacated space. From kick formation the offensive line may charge through without obstructing the defensive line, thus leaving the rush-line territory free for a receiver.

Passing to the side flat, in rear of, or along, the rush line is highly dangerous. Passing to the territory uncovered by a charging tackle or end, if the pass is made directly ahead, is, however, sometimes effective. The best passes are made to the receiver going to the open spaces down field. The receiver reaches this space by change of direction and pace, and he takes the ball going fast, generally turned in.

Passes cannot be made on the run. They

cannot be caught safely at extended speed. They are thrown on a fast traveling lob. If the receiver is unusually reliable, they may be shot like a baseball. They are generally thrown to a spot in advance of the receiver, the spot being dependent upon the speed and route of the receiver. Passes are always caught with the hands, like a baseball.

Delay is desirable. Two seconds' delay is necessary to make a good attempt from close formation. From open formation, the passer generally has all the time necessary with one protector. In close formation, this delay is obtained by the line holding. The backs spread and protect either side of the passer. In open formation the line need not block. Delay is obtained by the single protector in front of the passer. The passer may back off to the side. Plenty of time is available from the open formation.

The passer does not pass if he sees that the receiver cannot get the ball.

The passer and receiver should appreciate the fact that a ball thrown to an open space in advance of the receiver will result only, at the worst, in an uncompleted pass, provided the receiver is leading, by no matter how small a margin, the defensive backs.

The forward pass is a strong play. It is peculiarly strong as a scoring play. In the hands of greater individual excellence it is

Standard Deceptions

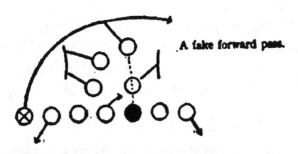

.A fake forward pass.

a rapid means of scoring. In the hands of inferior players it is a boomerang. Close to its own goal it is unusually dangerous to weak and strong alike.

Passing and receiving can be learned only by constant daily practice, under a good coach, from the beginning of the year.

When the direct pass is used and the distribution is such that the extra man is outside and behind the end, two receivers are available on that side of the attack. It will be seen that in this case the defensive wing back is in a serious dilemma if the two receivers run at him, one turning out and the other down the field. This is an important advantage resulting from the use of the direct pass.

Delay, secured by deception, will do much to strengthen the passing attack. For instance, some of the very excellent passers can fake a run, stop, and pass. A crisscross preceding a pass, with a delayed receiver running into an open space from which the defenders have been drawn by the other eligibles, can be used successfully.

THE ATTACK BY DECEPTION

The standard deceptions from the close and open formations are as follows:

1. The crisscross.
2. Split plays.
3. The hidden ball.
4. Delayed runs.
5. Quick kick.
6. Fake forward pass.

In addition, the fake kick is an important deception used from the open formation.

The old crisscross, where the back starts on an end run and passes the ball back to the end going in the opposite direction, is one of the best deceptions. It has a long history of success. Split plays, where part of the backs go in one direction and the others with the ball in another direction, have had little success. The defense is too quick to spot the ball. The "hidden ball" is executed in the same manner as a split play or a criss-cross. The transfer of the ball is hidden by the player passing, by keeping his back to the opponents, thus preventing them from seeing who really gets the ball for a small vital fraction of a second. Delayed runs and the fake forward pass both depend for their success on the defensive end failing to cross the line of scrimmage and spotting the ball. A good end very rarely fails to execute both these essentials of good end play. The quick kick is advantageous and necessary only

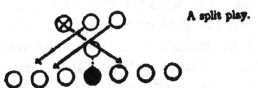

A split play.

when the defensive quarterback comes up to support the defensive backs. In such case, a quick kick over his head, provided it can be well executed, is a desirable play.

The really vital deception is the fake kick because it tends to protect the kicker and strengthen the kicking attack. A good fake kick is a run or drive that may be launched at any fast-charging line man or end who is hurrying the kicker. So used, it will tend to slow up that defensive player on his succeeding charges and thus give the kicker plenty of time to get his kick away.

Deceptions are all weak. Too many are ruinous. A fake kick, and possibly one other from the well-proved standard list, might be adopted.

UNUSUAL DISTRIBUTIONS ON THE OFFENSE

Unusual distributions on the offense may be disposed of by noting that lack of strength goes with lack of concentration. On running plays, delay of the ball behind the line is a weakness. Obvious forward-pass formations, which are without concentration, are always doomed to failure in rushing, through lack of concentration, and to failure in passing through the spreading of the defense.

SUMMARY

An analysis of the foregoing will show that a well-rounded attack should have eight running plays (four or five of which can be executed from open formation), a kick, three passes (one to the center and one to either flank), and one or two standard deceptions, one of which is the fake kick. Under no circumstances should there be more than these fourteen plays. If the character of the team and its development permit, the number may be reduced.

CONCLUSION

It may seem to many that the attack outlined in the preceding exposition is old fashioned and out of date. In many parts of the country, spreads, flying interference, sudden shifts of the rush line, and various other combinations are much in vogue. To those who believe that such complex formations make for success, a study of the history of the attack in football is recommended. The direct and simple assault of the defensive rush line has been the only form of attack that has yielded consistent success in football. For years, from 1890 until 1907, Yale was pre-eminent in the college football world. This pre-eminence was obtained and maintained by adhering to the simple direct assault. From 1908 until the present day, Harvard has wrested this pre-eminence from Yale by adopting the simple, concentrated, direct attack, whereas Yale has yielded her former glory the more readily by flirting with various jumping or spread rush lines, queer lateral passing, and other complex formations in defiance of her success and her history. There has been in the history of football but one successful attack, and that attack is the one that has been outlined above.

Success should follow simplicity of operation. The ordinary player—the problem of all coaches—is then free to concentrate on proving his individual superiority over his opponent, and it is on this individual superiority that the success of a team rests.

IV

THE DEFENSE

IT is necessary to turn again to the principles of war to obtain the proper conception of the defense in football. The defense is but a temporary expedient. It does not give us positive results. It should never be passive, however. Indeed, each defensive operation, in the classic defense, is a savage attack of the offensive play.

Three great principles underlie all successful defense. They are as follows:

1. When the attack concentrates, spreads, divides, or deepens, the defense does the same—that is, the center of mass of the defensive distribution is always opposite the center of mass of the offense.
2. The best defense is to foresee the play to be chosen by the offense and to concentrate quickly against it when the ball goes in play—that is, outguess the opposing quarterback.
3. A savage attack of the offensive play.

Balance the Attack

The classic distribution against the concentrated attack consists in placing seven

men on the line of scrimmage. The center of
this rush line is opposite the center of mass
of the attack. Behind this center and within
immediate supporting distance is a halfback.
Somewhat withdrawn on either wing two

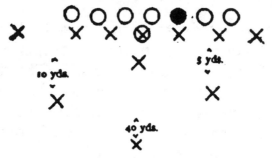

Normal defense against rushing attack.

other halfbacks stand. They are as close to
the line of scrimmage as they can get and
still feel sure of being able to cover a forward-pass receiver darting suddenly from the
offensive rush line. In the back field, at the
extreme range of the offensive kicker, is the
eleventh man on the team—usually the
quarterback.

The variations of this distribution depend
upon the attack formation. If a kick or open
formation is assumed by the offense, the defensive team must deepen also. If, instead
of a standard-kick formation, the offense

only partially deepens, the defense must do likewise.

One man sent out to the flank is balanced by the defensive wing back; two men by the end and back; three men by the tackle, end, and back. In each case the remainder of the defensive team shift their position so that the center of mass of the defensive distribution is opposite that of the offense.

Should the offense assume a formation with one, two, or three yards between the offensive line men, the defense does the same. In general, in this case the defensive line men charge through the interval and not at the offensive player. This charging is the reverse of that against a close concentration, where the defensive line men charge the man and not the interval.

There are three groups in all defensive distributions. The end, tackle, and wing back form a triangle on either flank, while the center of the defense is held by the two guards, the center, and the middle back. It is important that the triangular relationship of the tackle, end, and wing back be understood by the players, and that they be trained to realize that on the defense they are not individuals, but a group. For instance, should the end desire to drive in more quickly than usual, he should speak to the halfback and caution him to watch the outside. Should the tackle desire to break wide, he notifies the halfback; similarly, he notifies both end and half if he is going through inside. The center group has a similar dependent relationship. Communication between players in matters of this kind is generally by private signal or catch phrases.

In general, against the close formation the principle governing the position of any line man is that he uncovers from the ball all the ground he is able to protect. This generally results in bringing the defensive tackle opposite and not outside the offensive end.

It is vital that a defensive line man should not stand outside the territory he expects to protect and then charge into it. On the contrary, the history of successful line play shows that the defensive line man should stand well within the territory he expects to defend and charge out.

Following this procedure it is clear that the defensive line, in attacking any play, must operate as follows: The tackle charges over through or outside the defensive end and is responsible for the territory between the offensive end and tackle. He should get two to two and a half yards into the defensive territory. The guard charges over through or outside the defensive tackle and should get about a yard into the opposing attack. He is responsible for the territory between the offensive tackle and guard. The defensive center charges to the outside guard and is responsible for the territory between the offensive guards. This places the short-side defensive guard opposite the center, and he is responsible for the territory on either side of this center. It is assumed that the offensive center is so handicapped by handling the ball that this is possible. The short-side defensive tackle operates exactly as his fellow on the long side.

The result of this method of operation of the defensive line men is that the defensive line breaking through forms an arc inside the offense, with both tackles at its tips. This arc encompasses all plays of the attack.

If the play is directed at a particular line man, it will be seen that the line man is standing within the territory to be protected. By merely stopping his charge, fighting his way to the ground, and going under the play, he blocks its route. Moreover, his fellows, due to the policy of breaking wide, are coming directly to his assistance. The only unguarded hole has the middle defensive back directly behind it.

It is vital, whenever the attack begins to gain ground, that the defensive backs hit the play before it gets beyond the line of scrimmage.

Outguess the Quarterback

The players must be trained to figure, while on the defense, upon what play the opposing quarterback is about to call. The defensive team must understand the principles of generalship to such an extent that its members can make a reasonable guess as to what their opponents propose to do.

In order to stimulate the thought and action of one another, the defensive football team should talk like a baseball team. It is a good plan to encourage the ends and the backs to call the down and distance, and to caution one another constantly on what they think the next play is to be.

It is essential, and none too easy, to train the defensive team to recognize certain vital situations which require additional effort on its part. One of these situations is where the offense finds itself near the side line. The defense must realize that in this predicament one half of the possibilities of the attack are cut off. It is, therefore, of great advantage to hold the offense in close to the side line without letting it get outside. Similar positions are those where the attack is backed up on its own goal line. It sounds trite, but it is none the less of vital importance that the defensive team should realize its opportunity and endeavor by a supreme effort to hold the attack in just this fix and then try to block the kick, or at least make a fair catch and shoot for a score.

Either the center or the middle back should be required to change by signal the distribution of the back field, the roving center, and possibly one end. The man giving this signal must be sufficiently trained in field positions and the probability arising from a given down and distance, so that he can call the kick defense, forward-pass defense, or close defense with reasonable safety. However, a well-trained individual or group is above any signal system. They will, by constant co-operation and guessing of the opposing quarterback, shift their positions to meet the probable play.

5

It is customary, when expecting a kick, to drop the center back. His position, when dropped back, depends upon what the de-

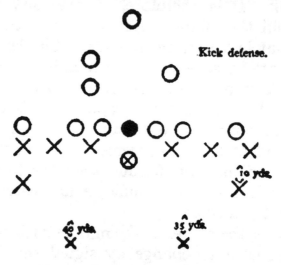

Kick defense.

fensive ends are to do, either one or both, about going through. The center also comes back on the forward-pass defense, and some times with one end.

The defensive back field should be in constant motion, if only for the purpose of misleading the opposing quarterback. For instance, a back may be able to draw a forward pass by coming up close to the line and then, as the signal is called, hurrying back to a safe position. This general method of operation also applies to defensive line work.

The defensive back field also changes position with the down and distance and the number of players in the back field. If the center drops back, the middle back and center divide up the defense behind their rush line. If one end stands flat or drops back, the remainder of the back field all move over to cover more securely the ground vacated by the opposite end when he goes through. Above all, all members in the back field keep shifting their positions and constantly guessing aloud the opposing quarterback.

When the attack has two eligible receivers on the end of the rushline, the closest cooperation must exist between the wing back and the middle back. The quarterback, in case this situation is very dangerous, must at times be ready to come up fast to help the wing back out of his predicament.

A SAVAGE DEFENSE

Paramount to all other features of the defense is that of an aggressive, attacking spirit. *The defense, above all, must carry the fight to the opponents.* This is accomplished by line men in the sharp, aggressive use of hands in breaking through. The backs must be taught

that when the attack is gaining ground they
must meet the runner before he passes the
line of scrimmage. The ends must not only
turn the play in, but they must also drive
into it—getting the runner or smashing the
interference.

A desperate attempt to block every kick
is an essential of good defense. Only an
excellently trained team can withstand a
determined onslaught on the kicker. A

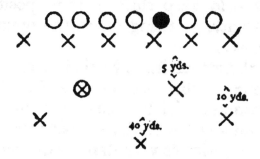

A forward pass defense.

blocked kick wrecks morale and often gives
the defense not less than half the field. Often
it wins a game. A determined attack on the
kicker always results in hurrying the kick.
This generally results in a short kick.

A savage attempt to block the forward
pass is the best forward-pass defense. The
rules permit a defensive player to launch him-

self into the passer while attempting in good faith to block the pass. This should be done if necessary. It is vital that the passer be compelled to throw the ball the moment he gets it.

There are certain features of defensive play on which there is considerable difference of opinion among leading coaches. One of the greatest of these is the method of playing defensive end. Some coaches have the defensive end, on all plays, drive straight into the back field. This has not been a very successful method. The classic method of end play has been to make the end responsible for the outside. He crosses the line of scrimmage three steps, slows the play up, and turns it in, and then gets the runner or the interference. The greatest ends have followed this method.

Another defensive feature over which there has been considerable difference among coaches is the method of line play. Many coaches require their line men to play with their weight on one or both hands and then to drive ahead straight, going under the offensive line. Given equal personnel, this method has generally failed. The traditional method of line play, which has met with success, is that in which the defensive player occupies the territory he is to defend and is trained to break through to the outside of his opponent—arresting his outward charge when he sees the play is at him, otherwise

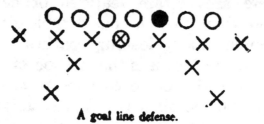

A goal line defense.

going through. This latter method requires more of the defensive player, develops him more, yields greater results, and is the way that the greatest players have played.

CONCLUSION

The defense in football, as in war, is but a temporary expedient. It is, of course, vital that the defense hold, otherwise it is difficult for the attack to play their kicking game or rushing attack as an offensive feature. Therefore, sufficient time must be put on defensive training to make it difficult for the attack to gain any ground in any part of the field, at any stage of the game.

EDWARD MAHAN, HALFBACK, HARVARD

V

POSITION PLAY

THE objective of all coaching is excellence in position play. Team work is the natural result of high-grade position play. The coach who depends primarily for team work upon well-drilled, co-ordinated group work is building his house upon sand. Good, reliable team work is the product of but one thing, and that is high-grade position play. Therefore, it behooves the coach to concentrate upon the individuals and to develop each to his highest excellence.

All really good football players have certain endowments without which it would have been difficult for them to succeed. These are brains, speed, co-ordination, and power. All are essential. All of us can recall plenty of great players who were decidedly lacking in one or another of these attributes. But their success was due to an unusual endowment of one of the other essentials and they were great in spite of the lack of any given one. There are a very few who seemed to have them all.

Certain positions on a football team demand, in addition to the essentials named, a certain amount of experience. Few backfield men can make good before acquiring several years of experience. It is rare, in the modern game, that an end or a center can learn to interpret properly in his first year the chameleon like changes of a football game. Experience is an asset hard to replace.

Quite often we hear inexperienced coaches complain of the lack of courage or sand in some of their players. The fault is not with the player, but with the coach. There is no quality so universal as courage when the players are handled properly. Any player properly handled will give everything he has for the success of the team. It is merely a case of expert management. A young line coach was noticed once to have discarded certain apparently very promising players. When asked about it he said: "They are no good. They are yellow." When pressed for an explanation, he said that he was showing them how to use their hands in breaking through; after arranging their heads just so, ·

he hit one of the neophytes a good jolt on the
jaw and sliced through. He then repeated
the formation, and if the player winced or
ducked on the second trial he knew he was
yellow and no good. So he wasted no more

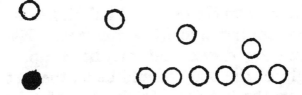

Freak formation: an attempt to overbalance the defense.
Surprise necessary.

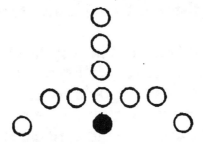

Freak formation: following the command "Hep," this distribution jumps to any normal or freak formation. Used
extensively in the West and South.

time on that particular man. If the successful coaches in the game of football had a
predilection for any such Spartan acid tests
as had this young coach, their successes
would have been few and far between. Any

coach who is worried about the sand of his men should consider how the white race, believing in its cause, went over the top during the World War.

End Position

The end on the offense should take a square stand on the line of scrimmage. His tail should be down and his head up. The weight of the body should be on the feet and not on the hands. He should not take position until the last moment, so as to worry the defensive tackle. When he takes position the distance from his own tackle should be varied.

When the ball goes in play he should make a quick, hard charge, followed up with short steps. At times he should make contact with his shoulder and sometimes with his elbow. Some ends have been quite efficient at driving sideways under a tackle's hands, hitting him with their hips, and crawling into him on hands and feet. In general, the tackle is attacked from the inside or outside, depending on whether an inside or outside tackle play is called.

On straight drives the end holds his ground momentarily, protecting the flank of the play.

When the line of the play is safe, the end drives through in front of the runner and takes out the first defensive back he can get to who threatens the play.

Good ends must be expert in leaving the line of scrimmage quickly when called upon to run with the ball. They must be drilled in taking the character of step which comes natural to them in getting away from the line quickly.

When called upon to receive the forward pass, he must get away from the line of scrimmage quickly at all costs. An end who allows the defense to check him on leading out for a forward pass has wrecked the pass. At all costs, the end must get away free. After leaving the line of scrimmage, the end leads out into the open space, receives the pass, and becomes an open-field runner—that is, he leads out into the open on a straight line, draws out the defense, and reverses the field or outruns it.

The pass should be caught with the hands like a baseball. One or both hands check the momentum of the ball, guide it to the body, and both hands then pin it there. It is then "fixed" under the arm, elbow and hand covering either point rigidly.

The skill which marks a good offensive end is that which always keeps the defensive tackle guessing.

When a kick is called, the end must move out so as to have an unobstructed start from the line of scrimmage. He moves away like a sprinter and after about fifteen yards he should verify the direction of the kick, swing to its outside, and bear down upon the catcher. Just before the ball lands, the end ordinarily slows up somewhat so as to have his weight well in hand in case the back tries to dodge or to reverse him. Sometimes it is good policy to tackle the catcher while going at full speed, just as he catches the ball. The end must be prepared to meet the opposition of the defensive back and he must remember that he is authorized to use his hands. At times the best defense is an attack of the defensive back. Some backs are trained to attack the end when he looks up to verify the flight of the ball or when he slows up to tackle. Forewarned is forearmed in such cases. Deception and proper use of the arms and hands will protect the end.

Defensive end play is reasonably simple. Against the running attack the defensive end goes straight across the line of scrimmage, meets the play with outstretched arms, slows it up, and turns it in. He takes as little ground from his tackle as he can, remembering that he is responsible for the outside. Having turned the play in, the end should drive into it from the flank, trying for the runner or all the interference.

He follows all plays on the opposite side of the line from behind, remembering that above all else he is a ball spotter. The end's first business, after crossing the line on all plays, is to spot the ball and guard against crisscrosses and other deceptions. It follows that he should be the man on the spot in case of a fumble.

Against the forward pass, the rule for end play is to hurry the pass. He must knock down the ball if possible, always jumping high at and in front of the passer. Considerable variation is permissible in end play against a forward pass. By signal he may stand flat and make himself responsible for short passes into his territory. In this case he must never let the receiver pass him. He should catch the ball if he can and knock it down, at all costs. Crowd the receiver, jump for the ball when necessary. It is vital that the ends vary their play to fit the occasion against a good forward-passing team. They must smell out the pass and notify their wing

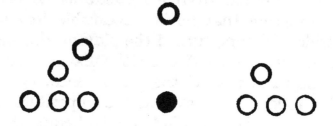

Freak formation: an attempt to scatter the defense and still retain concentration.

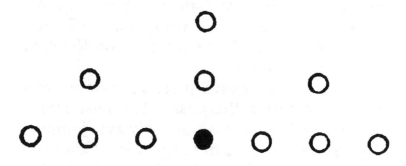

Freak formation: entire dispersion; all rushing strength sacrificed..

back by signal of whether they are going through or standing flat. Near the side line they have an excellent opportunity to take the shortest, straightest line to passer or kicker.

Against the kicking attack, the rule is for the end to hurry the kicker. This must always be so varied that a skillful quarter-back cannot figure exactly on what the end is to do. Near the side lines and close to the opponent's goal, the end generally goes straight to the kicker, working in conjunction with the tackle, and by signal cautioning the wing back to watch his territory and the outside. Sometimes the end may stand flat or even drop back off the line of scrimmage.

An end has considerable leeway in playing his position. He may break any rule provided he achieves the result. Above all he must remember that on the defense he is responsible for the outside. On the attack he must be a good receiver of the pass, capable at handling the tackle, and fast and effective down the field under a kick.

Position Play—Guards, Tackles, and Center

Before the forward pass was introduced into the game of football, it was a fixed and vital principle that if the line went forward the team won and if the line came backward the team lost. This principle in the modern game has its exceptions, but they are few and

far between. If nowadays an advancing line
does not always lead directly to a touchdown
by rushing, it always makes opportunities
and generally ruins the opposing attack.
This great underlying principle of offensive
and defensive line work should be engraved
on the heart of every line man. If the line
goes forward the team wins, if the line comes
back the team loses.

The line is the center of the battle. Skill
and knowledge of the game will help a line
man tremendously, but neither knowledge
nor skill will relieve line men of the rough,
hard fight which is the essence of football
and which begins, and often ends, on the line
of scrimmage. Above all, the line men must
be imbued with a spirit of punishing fight.
They must carry the fight to the opponents
and keep it there all the afternoon.

Line men should practice the art of concentration. To fight in a dream is as fatal
for them as it is for a pugilist. Eye and mind
must be trained to concentration. The underlying principle of eye concentration is
that it must be concentrated on the ball.
Some coaches will tell their men to watch
both ball and opponent. Never was a more
fatal error made. The eye cannot watch

two fast-moving things at the same time. To tell when the ball moves, the eye must be absolutely concentrated on it. On the defense, the line should always start with the ball. On the offense, the line may start with the ball or on verbal signal. In either case the line man must choose the object to be watched and concentrate upon it.

DEFENSE

The principle of defensive line work is to stand well in and to charge out, thus spreading and opening the offensive line. In general, the offensive line principle is the reverse of this. The line should make a wedge-shaped advance, keeping a close line.

The position of the defensive line man is analogous to that of a fighter stepping into a clinch or that of a wrestler starting a bout. Much of the best thought on line work has come from professional fighting and wrestling. The line man stands square on the line of scrimmage, with feet well separated. The weight and tail should be very low and the hands should be held still, but ready to strike in aiding the line man to break through.

Before taking final position the defensive line man should keep moving up and down

6

the line. Often it is a good plan to worry the opposing quarterback by lining up in rear of the man at his side and then jumping into position at the last moment. After having taken position, the feet should be shifted slightly in order to get the opponents

O Ball

Freak formation: players congregate and get signal for next play. They then jump to the new distribution and ball goes into play without signal.

guessing and thus break down their plans for charging.

There have been many famous methods of breaking through. Heffelfinger is said to have charged his opponent with his elbow, holding his hands locked while doing so. Brown had a tremendous uppercutting jolt which he used to turn his opponent aside. No line player ever played lower than Brown. His tremendous frame was drawn down like a powerful spring. When the ball went in play, he drove up and through his opponents, striking a powerful uppercutting jolt as he came. Bloomer was wonderfully quick, side-stepping as well as side-swiping with his hands. McEwen was exceedingly clever at guessing the point of attack and concentrating his charge on the face and head of the opponent nearest it. And so on, almost without limit, the special stunts of famous players could be cited.

There are, however, certain standard methods of leading. These methods are in a way as standard for line men as the methods of leading in boxing are for boxers.

The defensive line man may take a low position inside his opponent and make a straight charge with one hand on the throat and the other on the face, thus moving the opponent by steering his head. Or he may, in charging, step to the outside, striking a blow on the side of the opponent's head. Should the line man elect to take a low position somewhat outside his opponent, he may then charge straight ahead, striking one hand to the head and the other to the body. Or in this case he may side-step to the inside, charging with a blow to the inside of the head. An oblique charge in is bad.

When the defensive line man is not pressed, his position becomes more erect. Taking the erect position inside or slightly outside his opponent, he may practice the leads outlined above. The erect position at times offers opportunities for using both hands in catching the neck of a very low opponent.

The initial movement of the defensive line man with hand and leg is simultaneous. If the hands fail to clear the way for the legs, the player must be skilled in withdrawing his leg, stepping over or on his opponent, breaking through at all costs.

Once through the line, the defensive player must be careful not to go too far. His effort is absolutely wasted if he slices through the

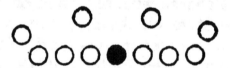

Freak formation: backfield scattered so as to get strength for passing. Runner exposed to defensive line.

play without doing any damage. He should be trained to stop and spot the core of the play. He should then wade toward it, getting the runner if possible, taking all the interference at least. By all means make it rough for the backs.

Against a standard-kick formation the defensive line should spread somewhat in order to give the tackles a clear shot at the back field. Driving straight through, they should knock the backs out of their path, drive through them, or step over them, and then make a desperate attempt to block the kicker by jumping in front of the path of the ball.

OFFENSE

On the offensive a line man should take a position with his feet well up under him. He should be crouched as low as possible, tail and weight away down, head up. One hand may touch the ground to balance with. The other arm should be bent, forearm and elbow in front of the body. In this crouched position there should be nothing exposed except knees and elbows.

This point should be made about the position of line men who have their feet well up under them. After initial contact is made between the two lines of scrimmage, the line man who has his feet under him is in a far more powerful position than the one who, for instance, has one foot or both well to the rear. The first is in the position of the fighter stepping into a clinch, the latter is out of balance and committed to a straight drive with his weight well in advance of its supports. The one has positive forces under him, the other has not.

There are several types of charge for the offensive line man. He may drive ahead with his shoulder, holding his forearms and elbows in front of his stomach. He may drive ahead with one elbow advanced and re-enforced by locked hands. Either of these methods may be used, either driving straight into the opponent or by dipping well under him. Should the defensive line man dive head-on under the play, the offensive line man must either walk on and over him or dip his leg under the dive before it gets to the ground. Once an offensive line man gets his knees under the shoulders of his opponent he can often walk him straight to the rear.

The great rule for an offensive line man is this: *He must either go forward or get out of the way.* If he comes backward he is a defensive player and a most effective one. The back never lived who could gain ground when his line came backward. The converse is also true. Any back can gain when the line goes ahead. But when the lines are a stand-off, it then takes a combination of excellent line and back-field play to produce results. The first principle in this combination is for the line man to give the back a chance by not obstructing his path. If the line man cannot go ahead, he must get out of the way.

The offensive line, on passing and kicking, should block without charging until the pass or kick is made. Under no circumstances must they permit an opponent to get through them.

It would be well for all line men to make themselves familiar with the following statement of line-play requirements and offensive and defensive stunts:

First Requirement: Discover and accustom yourself to that offensive position which gives best results in stability, quick starting, and a lifting charge. Such a position must be one in which the legs are well drawn up under the body; the body itself square to the front and inclined upward, with the buttocks close to the ground; weight resting on the toes, but balanced forward on a hand; and head up, with eyes open.

Second Requirement: Develop fast starting and hard charging. You should be able to throw your entire weight at an opponent in such a manner that when you strike him your legs are collected well under you, prepared for further effort. Speed is one of the most valuable habits in football, but to acquire a fast start from the crouching position of the line man requires constant training of mind and muscles. Get the habit.

Third Requirement: Practice using the hands and arms. You are allowed these on the defense in order to offset the natural advantages of the offense. Be sure that you take all that the rules provide. Use the hands and arms to keep away the opponent's body and for the purpose of shoving him right or left, up or down. It is not a game of tag.

Fourth Requirement: Concentrate your mind on the subject at hand. There may be said to be three distinct mental phases in the operations of a line man. Vision is centered correspondingly.

On Offense:

1. Getting the signal and deciding on the action required.
2. Starting with the ball or signal and starting fast.
3. After contact with opponent, a general cooperation in play of line.

On Defense:

1. Deciding on how you will go through.
2. Starting with ball and starting fast.
3. After striking opponent, forget him and go toward ball. You will shake off opponent unconsciously, but if you keep thinking of him you will stop and wrestle. Your object is to get to the ball.

Fifth Requirement: Play your defense game from the standpoint of the opposing quarterback. For instance, if it is third down and they have ten yards to go, you are fairly safe in looking for an open play. Of course, you cannot neglect your usual territory, but you can play a little wider and attempt to cover more ground. Tighten up as they get near your goal line, and in their end of the field spread out. In other words, try to regulate your game according to the attack you expect.

Sixth Requirement: Try to outwit your opponent. Make him think you are going to do one thing and then do the other. Don't hit him the same way every time. If he once becomes bewildered he will spend his time watching you and will forget to move. Football has a psychology of its own.

DEFENSIVE STUNTS

1. Strike opponent in face or shoulder for purpose of shoving him back.
2. Charge opponent in front or flank with elbows or forearms. (Heffelfinger and Hogan.)
3. Strike opponent on side of head or neck with either hand, charging through gap thus made. (Weeks made this result in a blow.)
4. Jump to side as ball is snapped and allow opponent to shoot by, helping him with your hands. (Bloomer.)
5. Grab opponent by headgear, neck, or clothes, and pull him through to either side as you charge through gap. (McKay.)
6. Slice through between opponents by turning sideways, using hands to assist.
7. Simply lift up opponent and throw him aside. (Can be used only against small man.)
8. Ram opponent into ground and vault over him.
9. Charge low, hug opponent's leg, put your shoulder in his belly, and throw him back.

CAUTION.—Under no circumstances allow yourself

to be thrown back. You simply lead the opponent's attack when you move backward and you interfere with your own secondary line of defense. If thrown off your balance, throw yourself to ground and spill as many opponents as possible by the use of your own arms and legs.

OFFENSIVE STUNTS

1. Use of elbows, with hands close to body to increase width of shoulders.
2. Use of knees in walking back a plunging opponent.
3. Dip charge—dipping under opponent and throwing him aside with head.

However, the best of all qualifications on offense is the fast charge which allows you to hit your man before he has started.

GENERAL RULE ON KICKS AND PASSES

Defensive:

1. Go through, attempt to block kick or pass, and at least hurry kicker or passer. Then keep after the ball and get it if loose, otherwise put out as many opponents as possible.
2. Use individual defensive stunts in eluding or knocking aside backs in attempt to block ball.

Offensive:

1. Do not charge, but hold long enough to provide necessary protection to kicker or passer. The proper amount of time must be learned by experience and study.
2. As soon as free, *sprint* down field, the line as a whole spreading out like a fan.

The last word on the work of the forwards is this: If the battle belongs to the strong, it is theirs because they represent the power of the team. Intelligent application of power takes brains, and no line man can rest content on physique alone. Football is a game of brains, and for its success it requires in the line of scrimmage not only power, but also mentality.

CENTER POSITION

There is little basic difference between successful center play and that of the other positions on the line. The center, however, both on offense and defense, has additional vital duties. On the offense he must pass, and on the defensive he is continually dropping out of the line of scrimmage to strengthen the protection against the pass, kick, or trick.

Every play starts with the center. The line cannot get into position until he has adjusted himself over the ball. He should take a square stance with his legs well apart. The guards and center should lock legs. Continual practice in adjusting the feet and weight is necessary to enable the three center men to lock legs and still obtain a low effective charge.

The paramount and vital duty of the center, the duty that comes before all others, is that of making a good accurate pass. Daily and painstaking drill is absolutely necessary. This drill can never be dispensed with. The older and more experienced the center is, the more he insists upon this daily drill.

In general the center makes three passes: a very short lob to the quarterback, a traveling float to the No. 3 back, and a quick spiral shoot to the kicker. The time element is important in all the passes. The ball must travel as fast as is consistent with safety. Accuracy is absolutely vital. Speed and accuracy in the long pass to the kicker will often speed up the kick by one half a second. The pass is generally made with a flip of the arms, wrist, and hand for the short pass and with a sharp shoot for the long pass. In this latter pass the fingers grasp the lacings and give the spiral motion to the ball as it leaves the hand. If the center has a tendency to pass over the head of the kicker, he should practice depressing the long axis of the ball as he shoots it to the rear.

It has been well said that the center is no better than his poorest pass and that one poor pass will lose a game.

On the defense the center should never leave his position in the line unless the line is holding. The distance he may take to the rear varies directly with the chances of success of a plunge through the line. On third or fourth down with five or more yards to go, the center should always get out of the line.

An especial effort should be made to drill the center on critical plays and positions. He may leave the line with impunity in one part of the field where it would be fatal to do so in another. If a center is wise, he can foresee the critical play and, by changing position at the last moment, he can ruin the attack. A good center shifting back and forth from line to back field and the reverse can worry a quarterback considerably.

It is true of all line men, but particularly of the center, that they can never handle any two situations exactly the same. Football is not played by rule of thumb. It is a game of brains; success follows the player and the team that make the fewest mistakes.

THE BACK FIELD

REQUISITES

The general requirements of a good back are experience, rugged physique, and speed.

Most important of these requirements is that of experience. Quite often we see line men developed in one season. This is never the case with a good back. A good back is a product of several years' experience. It is only through this experience that he learns to interpret and act instantly upon the chameleon-like changes of the football field.

There are two types of backs which should be on every team. The first is the heavy, hard-running, line-plunging back; and the second is the light, fleet, dodging, open-field runner. Both of these types should be capable in the field of the other.

Under the modern game it is also a necessity to have at least one back who can kick, run, and pass. With such a back the offense, from either the close or the open formation, holds a threat which compels the defense to keep well spread and on the watch for all variety of attack.

UNDERLYING PRINCIPLES

There are certain rules of back field play which may be classed as principles of play. They are as follows:

On the Offense:

1. Never run backward.
2. Run in climax. By this is meant, gather speed as you approach the line of scrimmage and hit the line with maximum momentum.
3. Run collected. By this is meant that a back should run with his chin and elbows tucked in and his weight well in hand, so that when necessary he can change direction.
4. Be dainty with your feet. Don't fall down. By this is meant that the back should be trained in that co-ordination which enables him to step over or on a pile without tripping, and that he should be so skillful in the use of his feet that it will be very difficult to throw him down except by a fair tackle.
5. On open-field play, lead out into the open, draw the defensive field, pick your opportunity, and reverse it by cutting back through the defensive players.
6. After passing the line of scrimmage, fix the ball under one arm and use the other hand and arm on the defensive players.
7. Speed is paramount.

On the Defense:

1. Talk to one another at all times, checking up on defensive territory and down and distance. Guess the quarterback.
2. If the opponents are gaining ground, hit the play before it passes the line of scrimmage.
3. Against a forward pass never let a receiver outside or by you. Play your territory as long as the receiver is in it. Cover the receiver in any

territory in which he is uncovered. When the ball appears, play the ball. Crowd the receiver to obtain your rights. Jump when necessary. Do not catch the ball on fourth down unless you can make a long gain. Be ready for a quick pass played in sequence.

4. Vary your position from the line according to the down and distance.

DRILLS

The following drills should be carried out through the season:

As soon as the backs arrive on the field they should spend about five minutes on individual drills. A quarterback should be required to pass the ball to the backs as they stand in front of a pile of sand bags one or two high. The back should start, receive the ball, go over the pile either by stepping on it or over it, and then should practice nosing off, turning, side-stepping, or dodging. It is a good plan to put several backs on the other side of the pile and require them to try to steal the ball. With a group obstructing the back as he comes over the pile, he is also trained in using his eyes to pick out the open ground between the players into whom he advances.

After each back has executed the above

drill once or twice, the backs should pair off and practice straight-arm work, reversing the field, and running down wide plays. After the completion of this they should be assembled by fours, pair against pair, and practiced in knocking down forward passes.

These individual drills should not be permitted to take over ten minutes at the most, but they should rarely be omitted.

GROUP DRILLS

The backs should then break up into two groups—the kicking and catching group and the forward-pass group. Where a back is both the passer and the kicker he should spend the appropriate time at each group drill. The operation of these groups has been explained elsewhere under "Drill." Having completed the kicking and passing work, the backs should be assembled for offensive-defensive group work. In this drill two teams without the lines of scrimmage are assembled for dummy work. The attacking group practices the particular plays necessary to advance the ball to the goal line. The defensive group adjusts its defense accordingly. Critical plays are made at full speed and the coach supervising the drill notifies the players

7

on such drills whether to permit their completion or not. This is necessary to avoid smash-ups. This particular group drill is very valuable in developing forward-pass defense, goal-line defense, and the execution of critical plays. It is obvious that all formations, plays, kicks, and tricks are executed and defended against in this drill. Following the individual and group drills teams should be assembled for dummy scrimmage.

THE ATTACK

A few general remarks should be made about the way a back should operate on the attack. When carrying the ball on an end run, a back should be careful to keep behind his interference and to carry the ball in the arm farthest removed from the, scrimmage line. He should turn inside or outside the end, depending on whether the end is turned out or in.

On a wide slant the same rule applies. On both the end run and the wide slant, once the back has passed the line of scrimmage he should lead out into the open and watch for his chance to reverse the field. On the close slant, the back should drive into the line, not with the idea of finding an opening, but with the intention of bucking the line. This play usually opens toward the center and the back must be ready to turn in toward the center the moment he sees open ground in that direction. On the close slant, as well as in all other plays, the back must be careful that he goes exactly where the play is called.

On straight drives, most backs hit the line high, with the chin tucked in and the body collected. Above all, on these plays they must keep their feet.

DEFENSE

On the defense a back is not only required to apply the principles stated above, but he also should work incessantly at increasing his effectiveness against the kicking game. He should take the offensive end out by himself when possible, and from time to time he should encourage the loose center or even the end to join him in waylaying the offensive end.

In conclusion, aside from the necessary experience, a back, to rise to high level, must have speed, fire, and drive. He should have all these requisites with enough intelligence to apply them effectively.

VI

DRILL

FEW coaches clearly realize the paramount importance of a carefully planned and organized drill schedule. The secret of good performance at critical moments is found in drill. No soldier ever benefited more by intensive and carefully planned drill than does the football player. It is through drill, and drill only, that the coach can make reasonably sure of good performance under great pressure.

The underlying principles of military drill and drill in football are the same. The striking analogy between war and football is once more made evident. Our Infantry Drill Regulations say that close-order drills are designed to inculcate that prompt and subconscious obedience which is essential to control, and that smartness and precision should be exacted in every detail. The same is true in football. Just as in war, we have the analogy of extended-order drills, combat exercises, and field exercises, all of which it is best to follow by "a brief drill at attention in order to restore smartness and control."

Drill should be of the kind that will not sap the player's vitality and which will yield him as much fun as possible and consistent. It should be executed at top speed only at intervals. Complete co-ordination of the eye, mind, and muscle should be taught at slow speed, then somewhat faster; and finally at intervals the individual or group should test themselves out at full speed. Easy drills co-ordinating eye, mind, and muscle, covering all the phases of individual, group, and team work, are the essential features of each day's practice.

SCHEDULES

A coach should lay out a general plan of development for his team which covers the entire season. The speed with which he develops his team depends upon the date of his most important game. Herewith is presented an outline of a general plan of development for a team which plans to play its final game toward the end of November.

Knowledge in position play	Sept. 7th—Dope sheets and tryouts. Sept. 14th—Mechanics of offense and position play. Sept. 21st—Mechanics of defense and position play. Sept. 28th—Kicking game, forward-pass defense, forward pass, and position play. Oct. 5th—Generalship, forward pass, and position play.
Precision and position play	Oct. 12th—Forward pass, kick advanced, precision in running plays. Oct. 19th—Defense and rushing game advanced. Oct. 26th—Defense kick and forward pass advanced.
Speed and fight	Nov. 2d —Rushing game and drive. Nov. 7th—Rush, kick, pass, and drive.
Spirit	Nov. 16th—Special situations; pass, kick, rush, and three days' drive. Nov. 23d —Condition and polish. Nov. 30th—Condition and polish.

It will be noted that this schedule provides for the assimilation of all the attack and defense in the first three weeks. The remainder of the season is devoted to raising the efficiency of the team by laying stress on individual or group excellence along various lines which, of course, differ with different teams. No effort should be made to adhere arbitrarily to any schedule. The

schedule should be changed as often as conditions demand.

Similarly, a weekly schedule should be compiled at the beginning of each week. The governing feature in making up this schedule is the amount of scrimmage to be prescribed for the team. A tentative weekly schedule for midseason should read about as follows:

Monday—No scrimmage. Light drills and dummy kicking scrimmage.

Tuesday—Short scrimmage, followed by drills and dummy forward-pass scrimmage.

Wednesday—Hard scrimmage. Rush, pass, and kick.

Thursday—Short scrimmage and drill. Forward-pass dummy scrimmage.

Friday—Short dummy kicking and catching scrimmage.

Saturday—Game.

Each day, however, the coach should write out and publish a detailed schedule of work for the day. A typical example of such a schedule is as follows:

Monday, September 26th

2.30 P.M.—Jones, Brown, and Smith will report early to the coach in charge of forward passing for extra practice.

3.00 P.M.—Everybody in blackboard room for critique on Saturday's game.

3.30 P.M.—Everybody on field. Backs at south goal post, line at north goal post, ends in center of field.

3.30–4.30—Individual and group work under position coaches.

4.30–4.40—As teams practice signals for ten minutes.

4.40–5.10—Dummy rushing and kicking scrimmage.

5.10–5.30—Specialists work at goal kicking, kick off, passing, etc.

5.30—Dummies, run, and in.

The above schedule merely blocks out the day's work in a general form. As a matter of application to a particular day and team, this statement of the day's work should be most detailed. All individual cases, for whom extra or special instruction or drill is desirable, should be mentioned. This daily schedule should be completed in time to furnish typewritten copies to each training table at luncheon. In this manner each player knows in advance the general or special layout of the day's work. It should be said here again that the coach must not hesitate to depart from the schedule when desirable. More often than not, it is best to take liberties with the schedule in the interests of working out a particular drill or sometimes even in the interests of harmony.

The head coach, having allotted the field and the time to the position coaches, must, together with the position coaches, see to it that the necessary time and space are apportioned to the necessary drills.

Basic Individual and Group Drills

There are certain individual and group drills in football which are basic and in which all must excel.

The basic individual drills are tackling and interference. These two fundamentals must be drilled daily at the tackling and interference dummies, under the close supervision of a coach. The time required is not great, but it is essential that the drill should never be omitted.

The basic group drills for the backs, ends, and center are kicking and catching, passing, center and quarterback, and the skeleton offensive-defensive group.

The basic group drills for the line are the starting signal, offensive line work, and breaking through.

The kicking and catching group should be carried on at the same time as the passing group. The kicker should be placed about ten yards from the side line and required to kick behind protection to the catchers. It is well to have unimportant players walk into the interference, so that all the conditions of a game will be simulated. A stop watch should always be used and the time taken from the

Organization of the

Field for Practice

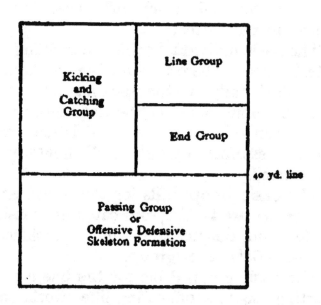

moment the ball is put in play until it hits the kicker's foot. Very little coaching of kickers, or, for that matter, of catchers, should be done. A kicker or a catcher either can or cannot perform with reasonable efficiency. If he cannot, the coach had better get some one that can. At times some of the ends join this group and practice leaving the line of scrimmage with the ball and closing in on the catchers. The catchers drill not only on actually catching, but also on how to play muffs, bouncing balls, and doubtful catches. They also drill on how to get the leading down-field end. In particular they co-ordinate with one another in crying "Mine," "Yours," or, "I have it," etc.

While the kicking and catching group is at work, the forward passer should be practicing throwing his different passes. He can keep a large group of receivers busy at this work, as the receiver often takes the ball on the dead run. Too much of this sprinting work, however, will soon overtrain a player. Here again the stop watch should be in constant attendance, and the passer should have simulated protection and opposition. It is often well to have a couple of defensive backs operating with the ends or backs receiving the pass.

Both of these groups should set aside, every few days, a half hour in which to move about the field, practicing their kicks, catches, and passes in different field positions. In general, however, the kicker should practice on his own goal line, with his foot about ten yards from the side line. The passer should do likewise in general practice on the opponent's twenty-five-yard line. Both of these positions are obviously critical.

After the completion of the work in the kicking and passing groups, all the backs and some of the centers should be assembled for offensive-defensive skeleton group work. The ends should join this group when it is not essential that they work with the line or by themselves.

The offensive element of this skeleton group takes the ball at midfield and advances the ball by various plays to the goal line. The work is done either at a jog trot or at a walk. Critical plays, such as forward passes and drop kicks, are executed at top speed. It is desirable very often that the offensive element be directed from the quarterback position by the coach. He may then drill the offense on all the plays necessary, and at the same time watch for his opportunity to catch the defense off balance.

It is apparent that as the offense drills in the execution of its attack, so the opposing defensive skeleton group is drilled in defense work. It is important that the defensive center be in this group. Of course, the offense and defense exchange places after a while.

The skeleton group just outlined above is one of the most valuable group drills in football.

There is, finally, a small basic group which must also drill together incessantly. This group is made up of the center and quarterback. Only by constant practice and association can the center and receiver become absolutely accurate in transmitting the ball to the backs. Indeed, so important has the work of the center become in modern football that it seems as though it would be best to separate the center for a drill by himself each day while the other individual and group work is going on. This drill of the center should cover all kinds of passing.

It has been well said that all plays start with the center and that he is no better than his worst pass. It is a very interesting study to analyze the effect of bad passing on kicking or forward passing. It will be found that accurate and fairly swift passing is one of the vital ways of speeding up these critical performances.

It will be noted in the discussion of these drills that it is assumed that a squad of about fifty—say four elevens—are available. Of course, the coach should direct the work of at least one group with the idea of developing the first-string men.

The first basic group drill for the line is that of the starting signal. The offensive starting signal is primarily for the use of the line. Each day, or every other day, the line coach should have the various rush lines assembled in their proper positions and practice starting by signal. Five minutes of this, every other day, will keep the line men in first-class practice starting with the signal. Care must be taken to see that the center does not allow the line to beat the ball.

The second important group drill for the line is that of offensive line work. In this group, the ends may or may not be present. Two lines are placed opposite each other, and while one line simulates breaking through, the other line practices its assignments on particular plays.

The defensive line is the third basic-line group drill. The work is so hard that it is preferably taught with four lines operating. Two lines face each other and the defensive line actually breaks through when the ball is put in play. After doing this once or twice, it is best to have this group replaced by two other lines that perform for the edification of themselves and the first two lines that stand as spectators.

In this offensive and defensive line work all the detail of position play should be thoroughly thrashed out.

LIST OF DRILLS

The preceding basic group drills have been described sufficiently to bring out the point that they cover the basic and critical operations of a team. Teams that can perform these operations well will probably play good football.

It is necessary to realize that perfect drill does not in itself guarantee high excellence. The team work of the great teams in the history of football was not based upon drill.

The excellence of our greatest teams—indeed, it might be said of all teams—arises from the excellence of the individual players. Teams are great and the team work is there because of this individual excellence.

Therefore, too much importance cannot be attached to those drills which develop the individual. They are too numerous and too various to be gone into in this book, but a sufficient number will be outlined for each position to enable any coach to choose some or to devise others which may be applicable to his players.

DRILLS FOR ENDS

OFFENSE

Individual

1. Sprinters' start.
2. Short races.
3. Long races.
4. Position on line on offense.
5. Interference dummy.
6. Catching passes.
7. Dodging.
8. Holding ball.

Group Work

1. How to run down under kicks.
   (a) Last end of run.
   (b) Getting past a man trying to block.
2. Running down under kicks with and without tackling.
3. Boxing tackle.
4. Working with tackle, and with tackle and halfback, in ways of disposing of defensive opponent.
5. Forward passes.
6. Special situations and field positions.

DEFENSE

Individual

1. Tackling dummy.
2. Very easy live tackling.

3. Falling on ball. Picking up ball.
4. Stealing ball.

Group Work

1. Defense against end runs, open and close formations.
2. Defense against skin tackle.
3. Defense against forward passes.
4. How to block an end going down under kicks.
5. How to block kicks.
6. Special situations and field positions.

DRILLS FOR LINE

Shifting along line (offense), (which man to take).
Shifting along line (where to be), (defense).
Diagnosing plays (end runs, passes, line drives, splits).
Going down on kicks.
Dummies.
Stance.
Breaking through (stance, use of hands, body charge).
Plays once removed.
Falling on ball.
Light line tackling.
Catching man in open field.
Dodging.
Sprints.
Easy use of hands.
Special situations (goal line, side line), (end through).
Starting signal drill.
Tackle and end (offense and defense).
Blocking a kick.
Critical situations.
8

DEFENSIVE DRILLS FOR TACKLES AND GUARDS

Low position inside	Straight charge—one hand to head, other on face.
	Side-step to outside—blow on side of head.
Low position outside	Straight ahead—one hand on head, other on body.
	Side-step in—blow on inside of head.
	Oblique charge in—bad.
Erect position inside	Straight ahead—one hand to head, other on face.
	Side-step to outside—blow on outside of head.
	Oblique charge out—blow on inside of head.
Erect position outside	Straight ahead—one hand on neck.
	Side-step in—blow on head or catch neck.
	Oblique in—bad—one hand on neck, other on body.
Position Exercise (both erect and low)	Use hands each time.
	Stand inside—side-step out.
	Stand outside—side-step in.
	Feint one way and go other.

OFFENSIVE DRILLS FOR TACKLES AND GUARDS

1. Protecting the line of the play on an end run or wide slant.
2. Turning opposing guard in on close slants.
3. Wedging on straight drives.

4. Passing opponent along from point of wedge.
5. Going through on secondary defense.
6. Avoiding good defensive hand work.
7. Against a plunging defense, use of legs, and stepping on or over.
8. Square stance and short steps.
9. Blocking for kicks.

DRILLS FOR CENTER

1. Passing to quarterback, kicker, and No. 3 back.
2. Starting signal drill.
3. Co-operating in offensive and defensive line drills.
4. Co-operating in defensive back-field drills.
5. Forward-pass defense and kick defense.
6. Critical offensive and defensive situations.

DRILLS FOR BACKS

BACKS

1. Fixing ball and starting.
2. Picking up ball, going over pile, nosing off, turning, side-stepping, dodging.
3. Straight arm and defense, reversing field.
4. Running down wide run.
5. Coming up on line plays and wide plays.
6. Spoiling forward pass. (This work is done in pairs, and in skeleton open and close formations.)
7. Short kick.
8. Field positions, side lines, inside opponent's ten-yard line, inside own ten-yard line.
9. Kicking, catching, kicking defense.
10. Each particular play, defense.

11. Each back, immediately upon coming on the field, will get a partner and practice for five minutes individual stunts as follows: over bags, nose off, turn off, dodge, side-step, straight arm, reverse field, run down wide plays, knock down forward pass.

QUARTERBACK

As above and

1. Working with center with ball and signals.
2. Drilling on field positions, downs, and distance.
3. Scoring play.
4. Voice and bearing drill.

The drills of the individual and group are followed by dummy scrimmage, which is applied to all situations and phases of the game. It is important that a dummy kicking scrimmage end the week. For those to whom the term "dummy scrimmage" is new, let it be explained that it refers to simulated play at reduced speed in which two teams engage. The defense is cautioned not to tackle and not to oppose violently. Critical plays, such as passes and kicks, should be played at full speed. In this case, the defense should be especially cautioned not to bump the offensive player.

In conclusion, let it be said that the importance of carefully planned and skillfully organized drill cannot be overestimated. It is the secret of good performance. There is one caution, however, that should be given and that is: Do not drill the individuality or initiative out of your players. Drill should never be hidebound nor arbitrary. The player should at all times be encouraged to control the drill himself. The real stars of the game of football have generally been men who did drill themselves to the high degree of excellence they obtained. Under no circumstances must either the drill itself or the drill-master dominate the player. On the contrary, the player must be encouraged to control the drill and to rise above the coach and the coaching. In this manner only is high individual excellence obtained.

VII

THE KICKING GAME

A GOOD kick is an indispensable part of the offense. A mediocre kick, properly used, can do wonders. Even a poor punt skillfully used is a tremendous strength to either attack or defense.

The writer is well aware that the basis of some football systems requires that the ball shall be kicked only as a last resort. The general theory of such an attack is that the opponents cannot win if they never get hold of the ball. Such a theory is all very well where one team has a very considerable advantage over another. This condition does not exist when equal personnel and skillful coaching oppose each other. Under these latter conditions the history of the game of football shows that the rushing and passing attack comes to a standstill and the issue turns on the breaks in the game. These breaks are developed best through the skillful use of the kicking attack.

Moreover, the use of the kicking attack is one of the great offensive weapons, and a coach cannot afford to disregard it in the development of his team. The statistics of most big games which have been equally contested show that the contests hinge in many respects upon the skillful application of the kicking game. The statistics of Harvard-Yale games and Army-Navy games and most other equally contested big games show that the number of kicks in such contests will range from thirty to fifty by each opponent per game.

THE KICKER

A kicker cannot be made. Many good kickers have been ruined by unnecessary and ill-advised coaching. Good kickers are generally the result of continued practice throughout preparatory-school days. Each individual kicker has a form of his own, and any attempt to change his form generally results disastrously. As long as a kicker is giving good results it is best for a coach to confine himself to suggestions, which the player may or may not use, as he sees fit. When the kicker is not giving the desired results, it is generally best to point out where he should show better results and then watch to see if the kicker can get the results himself. If this plan does not work, or even in the beginning, a skillful coach of kicking can point out the part of the kicking performance which the kicker might improve on.

General Theory of the Kicking Game

In theory, the kicking game is greatly strengthened by kicking from the center of the field toward the side lines, provided that the kicker is skillful enough to do so. The

A Method of Blocking a Kick

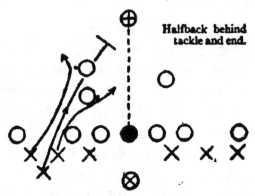

Halfback behind
tackle and end.

quarter should bring the ball to position in midfield, and the kicker should try to land the ball in the vicinity of the side line. The kicking team should then hold the opposing attack close to the side line and compel them to kick from its vicinity. Thus the opposing kicker may kick out to the center of the field, thereby giving the catcher a good opportunity for a free run in the open. What is worse, he may kick the ball outside well within the limit of his kick. Thus the kicking attack may advance down the field either by outkicking, run-backs, or by the breaks in the game.

It must be understood that this statement of kicking from the center to the side is highly theoretical. The success of the kicking game is no way dependent upon it. A good kick straight ahead is quite sufficient for the successful prosecution of the kicking game. However, when a team is blessed with a highly efficient kicker, the application of this theory will help tremendously.

One of the great rules of quarterback play is to *press the kicking game. Play for and make the breaks.* In a close contest, the kicking game leads to the breaks. A poor catcher in the back field, a slow kicker, a bad passer at center—any one of these weaknesses or others may develop. Under hard smashing the opponents will crack and the opportunity for a score will appear. It is then that the rushing attack, the forward pass, and the scoring kick become effective. *Work for the opportunity and then make good* is one of the great axioms of the game of football.

Technique of Kicking

The kicking performance may be divided into the following parts: receiving the ball, handling the ball, dropping the ball on to the foot, the swing of the leg, the manner of holding the foot, the steps preliminary to the swing.

In receiving the ball, the kicker should stand not less than eight yards back for a quick performer and not more than twelve yards back for a slow performer. Ten yards back is about the usual distance. He should stand with his weight evenly on both feet, but ready to shift it quickly to the foot not used in the first step before kicking. His body should be square to the front. Many kickers extend both arms, hands, and fingers outstretched, ready to receive the ball.

When the ball strikes the hands an important part of the kicking performance is the quick manipulation of the ball in the hands to bring the lacings up and to extend the ball ready to drop it on the foot. A good drill for this is obtained by tossing the ball a few inches into the air, quickly adjusting it the moment it strikes the hands, and then going through all the motions of kicking.

Dropping the ball accurately on to the foot is the next vital step. By many kickers, the ball is best placed on the foot by balancing the ball on one hand while extended. It should come accurately on to the outside of the foot, lacings up, long axis either parallel to the long axis of the shoe or slightly turned in. *The eye of the kicker should be kept constantly and vigilantly on the ball.* More kicks are spoiled by failure to place the ball accurately on the foot than from any other cause.

When the ball starts on the fly-back from center to the kicker, the kicker should *start* to prepare himself to kick. Many kickers are ruined by prescribing set steps for them to take. Kickers vary considerably in the steps they take before kicking. Some step back with their kicking foot, then forward with the off foot, and then kick. Some take two long steps forward and then kick. Some, with quick hitching steps straight up and down, kick from their tracks.

The leg swing is best made at about an

angle of from thirty to forty degrees to the side, although a few kickers kick straight to the front. The foot is held tense at the moment of hitting the ball, with the toes depressed. It is important that the toes be kept depressed and the foot rigid. The kick should be firm and as powerful as possible without deranging its accuracy. The foot, when striking the ball, should pass under it in a slight arc, which will give the ball the spiral rotation.

VITAL POINTS

Several important points should be made about the coaching of a kicker and the kick itself.

In the first place, the most important thing about the kicking performance is to get the ball off. It must not be blocked. This means that the kicker, when pressed, must be able to kick inside of two seconds by the stop watch. A kicker should be able to tell on each separate kick just how much his opponents are pressing him. The acme of good kicking is to kick at the last moment, thereby allowing the ends to get down the field. This is a dangerous proposition for all except the most experienced and should not be coached. When a kicker is kicking slowly, the best thing for the coach to do is merely to say, "Kick faster." When the kicker goes too far forward, the best thing for the coach

Another Method of Blocking a Kick

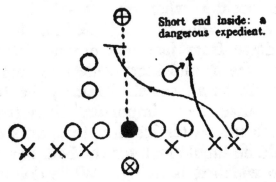

Short end inside: a dangerous expedient.

to do is to make a mark on the ground and tell the kicker to kick behind the mark. The manner of kicking faster or arranging not to go forward should be left to the kicker. He may be encouraged to experiment. Coaching that affects the kick in consistency or distance should be stopped at once.

END WORK

The second element of the kicking game is the covering of the kick. This is the most important work of an end, and no end is available material if he is unable to cover kicks properly. An end should vary the position from which he starts down the field. In general, he should start down far enough out so that he is sure to be on the outside of the opposing back field. At times he may start down from in close—that is, from his regular position when on the attack. This, however, is dangerous. If skillful, he may start down from just outside the defensive tackle. He should start wide and turn the catcher in at all costs. Making the tackle is, of course, more important than turning the back in. After his first ten yards down the field he should look for the ball, to see the side to which it is flying. While doing this he should be careful not to allow the defensive back to get hooked up with him. When going down the field, the same as on the defense, a good end has his hands and arms ready for immediate use for getting by the defensive back.

An end should be careful not to overrun the opposing catcher. By this is meant, running full speed the full length of the kick and trying to negotiate and tackle the catcher without slowing up. A good end generally slows up as soon as he sees the catcher getting the ball. He then starts to make the tackle with his weight and speed well in hand. Overrunning on the part of an end generally results from the kicker outkicking his ends—that is, kicking so far that the ends feel they must go full speed to keep up with the ball. It is a mistake on the part of the end to try to keep up with the ball by overrunning, but it is a far worse mistake for the kicker to indulge in low, long kicks that cannot be covered. The kicker should always kick to his ends, with the privilege of trying, at times, to sift in a long, low one over the heads of the back field. The kicker can, of course, prevent over-kicking by increasing the height of his kicks.

RECEIVING THE KICK

Good back-field work on the receiving end of the kick is essential.

Catchers cannot be developed by coaching. A back can either catch or not. If not, he should be gotten rid of at once. It does not pay to coach a catcher very much. He should, however, have daily practice to keep himself in good shape. Most players catch by checking the momentum and steadying the ball with one hand. This hand guides the ball to the body, where it is pinned by both hands and arms. High kicks are the most difficult to catch. In this case, one hand should be kept under the ball. Most good catchers guide the ball with the hand that checks its flight to their chest, pinning it there with both hands.

The second back-field man should back up on all bounces and on all kicks the catching of which appears doubtful. When he does not back up, he should hang well out to the flank of the first down-field opponent. He should smash into this opponent at about an angle of ninety degrees, crack him either in the head or in the body with as much momentum as he can gather with safety to himself. This method of taking out a down-field end will often scare an end for a whole game.

SKELETON KICKING FORMATION

The kicking group should operate every day. Service conditions should be simulated. The kicker should kick behind protection, and ends should go down on a catcher without tackling. Defensive halfbacks should be used from time to time. The opposing ends and tackles should be simulated. Without trying to block the kick, they should walk through on the protection, thereby reproducing all the elements of a game. Substitutes should be used in this work to simulate these conditions.

It is absolutely vital that a stop watch be used to time the kicker during this drill. The kicker must always kick in less than two seconds from the time the ball goes in play.

It is desirable from time to time to put the catchers under pressure by yelling at them as they receive the ball.

On Fridays and Mondays a certain part of the dummy scrimmage should be devoted to the exchange of kicks.

FAKE KICKING

There is a principle in the use of the fake kick that the quarterback should understand thoroughly. When the kicker is pressed, the quarter should immediately drive a fake kick at the opponent who is hurrying the kicker. Both quarter and kicker should be on the watch to determine what opponent this is. There should not be many fake kicks. A few drives through the line, similar to those from the close formation, are sufficient. It will be found that the skill-

9

ful use of the fake kick will arrest opponents who are threatening the kick.

DROP KICKING

Drop kicking is a highly specialized performance. The kicker should rarely kick from his own break. He should secure the services of a center, and the coach should time each kick. The kicker, glancing at the goal, passes an imaginary plane through the center of the goal posts and his foot. He notes where the trace of this plane cuts the ground immediately in front of him. He receives the ball, adjusts it, and drops it along the line of this trace previously marked on the ground. Some drop kickers actually draw a line along the ground, marking the direction of the center of the goal posts. It is vital that the kicker be skillful in adjusting the ball before he drops it. Most drop kicks that fail are unsuccessful because the ball is improperly adjusted or carelessly dropped. Just as in punting, the kicker must always keep his eye on the ball when kicking.

CONCLUSION

The above outlines the machinery of the kicking game. It is simple, but its importance cannot be overestimated. Played in combination with a good running attack, it should land the attacking team within striking distance at least two or three times in a game. The score can then be effected either by the rushing game, the drop kick, or the pass.

Once again the attention of the reader is invited to the history of close contests. Such games will show that the running attack against an equal opponent fails until the opponent's condition or morale has been broken. If their endurance and determination remain good throughout the contest, scores are effected most readily by the kicking game. The history of close contests is offered in testimony of this fact.

VIII

THE FORWARD PASS AND ITS USE

THE most interesting element of the attack in the modern game of football is the forward pass. The spectator enjoys this play more than any other. It gives the player and coach a splendid gamble with which to advance the play. Were it not for the forward pass, the game of football would be more or less of a mathematical proposition. With the forward pass, the element of chance and speculation is tremendously increased.

Certain facts concerning the forward pass have been developed during the few years in which it has been authorized. In the first place, an offense which rests entirely on the forward pass is a failure. It is a proven fact that when the defense knows the pass is to be made (no matter what the distribution of the offense may be) the defense can fully defend against the pass. The best illustration of this fact is found in the experiences of the Canadian players when they came to certain American colleges for the purpose of illustrating the possibilities of passing under

Forward Pass Areas

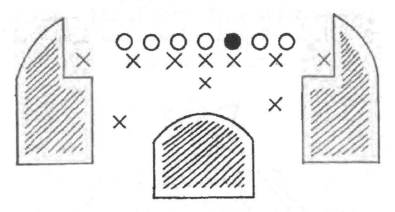

The successful execution of a pass depends upon the receiver arriving uncovered at an open space. The open spaces in the normal defense are indicated above. Similar diagrams may be worked out for the defenses of any opponent.

the British game. These men were professionals and had developed passing to a point far beyond anything seen in the American game. Nevertheless, the American defense was fully competent to handle their passing. It is said that the Canadian players completed pass after pass laterally and backward, but were unable to advance the play down the field by this method. Most coaches and players can, from their own experience, cite cases of teams unusually skillful in the pass which were unable to gain victories because the offense was limited to skillful passing alone.

Indeed, it has been found that the forward pass cannot be used generally and with impunity on all parts of the field against a

The Attack by Passing

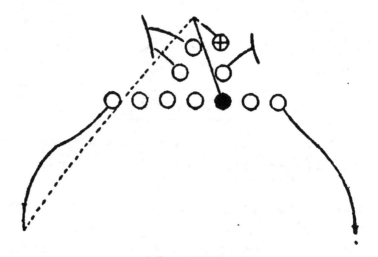

A Downfield Pass

strong defense. Given a strong defense, the chances are two to one against the success of the forward pass. It can be readily understood that the offense, in its own half of the field, is unwilling to take this chance of losing the ball. The forward pass, then, is

reserved in general for use in the opponent's half of the field when the normal methods of attack have failed. It is, of course, necessary to foresee the failure of the attack and to make the pass before the defense have realized that the attack is stopped.

We may say, then, that the forward pass is a very strong, critical play or gamble. In

The Attack by Passing

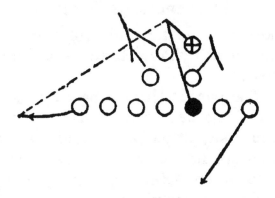

A Flat Pass

general, it should never be thrown inside the attacking team's forty-yard line. Its use is confined to midfield and the territory of the opponents. It is an exceedingly strong gamble for a score. In the prescribed territory, a strong forward-passing team may often mix the forward pass with the running attack in an exceedingly dangerous fashion. Most of us have seen defensive teams whose forwards have been demoralized by the failure of the backs in defending against the pass. In this case, the running attack immediately begins to advance. Forwards must realize that their best method of defending against the pass is to crash through and hurry the passer.

PRINCIPLES OF PASSING

There are certain principles in forward passing which have been established by experience:

(a) The pass is thrown best by the No. 3 back. It has been found that he has more time than any other player and that, due to his position, he can be used as a passer at any place where delay is gained by deception.

(b) The pass should be a traveling lob, not a shoot. A shoot is far too difficult to handle or to throw with the required accuracy.

(c) The ball should be thrown over the end or halfback. | It should arrive and hang over his face when he looks up, floating or traveling through the air like a ripe plum ready to be picked. | The receiver should catch with his hands as in baseball. The ball may be steadied and guided to the body when necessary, as in the case of catching a punt.

(*d*) In general, the ball should lead out the receiver into an open space, so that the receiver can take the ball on the run without materially slowing up. The receiving end of the attack generally goes down outside the defensive tackle, changes direction after passing the wing back, looks for the ball, keeps on running, at the proper time again looks for the ball, and finally receives it going with speed held in slight check.

(*e*) The ball is thrown with the long axis parallel to the ground or slightly tilted up. In throwing, it is best to teach the passer not to grip the ball.

(*f*) The effectiveness of the pass is greatly increased when it is thrown as a surprise on a quick lineup.

FORWARD-PASS PLAYS

The following general types of forward-pass plays have been used more or less successfully:

(*a*) The receiving end or back both going out wide to the open space or both going straight down field to the middle open space, or where there are two receivers on the same side, one going out and the other going down. The pass with two eligibles against the same defensive wing back is exceedingly hard to defend against.

(b) Passes in which the receiver cuts diagonally across the defensive back field, taking the ball over the inside shoulder.

(c) Passes in which receivers, as stated above, lead the defensive backs away from the territory, and then the real receiver, somewhat delayed, comes into that territory, taking the ball after the defenders have been drawn away.

(d) Some teams have developed certain special formations for the forward pass. These formations have been so constructed that a strong running attack behind a rush line is attempted, while at the same time a group of forward-pass receivers hang on or off the line of scrimmage well out to the flank. The running attack of such teams has generally failed, due to lack of concentration. Some other teams have practiced sending their entire rush line through and down field on forward passes with some success. Ordinarily this method sacrifices the protection of the passer, which, in a close contest, is vital.

It may be said that any scheme of forward passing must be so conceived that the passes will be made from the normal close and open

The Attack by Passing

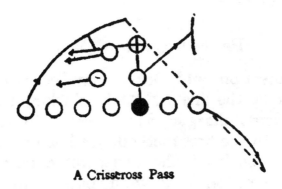

A Crisscross Pass

formations. If this is not done, the basic element of the attack is sacrificed, and the defenders may loosen up and distribute themselves successfully against the pass.

DECOYS

A vital element in the forward-pass play is the work of the players whose duty it is to decoy the defenders away from the receiver. These men must be exceedingly keen about leading out at full speed in a manner exactly similar to that in which they would go if they were to receive the ball. In addition,

they must call for the ball by shouting or by
such other outward manifestations as the
situation may demand and as are calculated
to mislead the defense. A coach cannot be
too particular about training players in their
work as decoys.

PROTECTION AND DELAY

Protection and delay may be obtained
either by the line and backs blocking fast all
opponents charging the passer or by deception. In the first method, the line and backs
should block for the two seconds necessary
to accomplish a forward pass from close
formation. If the element of surprise is
properly handled by the quarterback and the
pass is thrown from a quick lineup, this delay
and protection are readily obtained. Moreover, in this case the receivers have no trouble
passing the line of scrimmage and often
pass the defending backs before the latter
are alive to the situation. Protection and
delay may also be obtained by deception.
The good old-fashioned crisscross is an
excellent method of obtaining a standard
deception with a forward pass. A highly developed forward-passing team may also

secure this delay and protection by first
making a lateral pass and then a forward
pass.   With delay secured by deception the
offense is enabled to throw one of the most
dangerous of the forward passes, the so-called

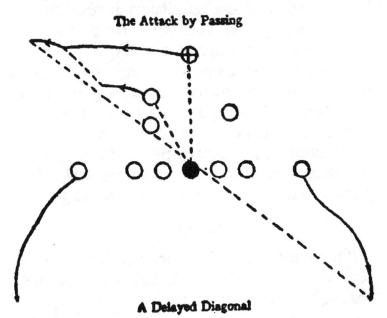

The Attack by Passing

A Delayed Diagonal

delayed diagonal.   In this case, the deception
or lateral pass leads the defenders and the
decoys to one flank, while the delayed receiver slips well out and down on the other
flank.   The delayed pass is a long throw
diagonally across the field to the receiver.   It
is an exceedingly effective forward pass.

Passing from Open Formation

It often happens that the offense has great difficulty in getting off its passes from the close formation. Quarterbacks should be trained to realize this situation and should throw their passes thereafter from the open formation. Although the defense is opened out against the pass when the offense is in open formation, nevertheless, a good back, threatening kick, pass, and run from the above formation, can at times consummate successfully the forward pass. Passing from the drop-kick formation is particularly dangerous to the defense when close to its goal.

Drills

There are two drills in connection with the forward pass which should be practiced throughout the season:

(a) Passing.

The passer, with receivers and substitutes, should assemble at the various critical positions on the field and the passer should practice throwing the ball on his different plays to the various receivers. It is imperative that a stop watch be used in this drill in order that the passer be required to throw within the required time limit of about one and three fourths seconds. In this drill the passer not only learns to throw, but also to vary the ball thrown for the particular receiver and play.

(b) Forward-pass Defense Play.

This drill is practiced in skeleton formation without the rush line. The attacking element varies the passes and rushes for the purpose of catching the defense off balance. The defense must be required to practice the following elements of forward-pass defense:

1. Learn to be ready for the pass play to come in quick sequence. Don't be caught napping.
2. The best safeguard is to guess when the quarterback is going to throw it. Opponents stopped in the beginning of the game, third or fourth down. Always a possibility that they will throw on first or second.
3. Opponent's attack stopped, one end at least must be prepared to re-enforce the back field. Ends bone this.
4. The center must be careful about getting out of defensive position.
5. The line must hurry the pass.
6. The defensive back field must never let a man outside or by.

7. Play your territory as long as the receiver is in it. Cover the receiver in any territory in which he is uncovered. When the ball appears, play the ball.
8. Crowd the receiver to get your rights.
9. Sometimes it will be necessary to jump.
10. Catch the ball if you can; beat it down, at least.
11. Talk, talk, talk.
12. If ball is sure to strike ground, don't catch it on fourth down unless you can make a long gain.

The items on forward-pass defense given herewith, which refer to the line, should be the subject of drill under the line coach.

TYPICAL AND CRITICAL SITUATIONS

From time to time, during dummy team work, the two teams should be taken to typical and critical positions on the field, and the forward-pass plays and defenses should be practiced.

CONCLUSION

Experience has shown that the vital element in the forward-pass game is the efficiency of the passer. The success of the forward pass is 90 per cent dependent upon the passer. A good forward passer can throw a ball which any fairly good receiver can handle. A good forward passer at times becomes so efficient that it is extremely difficult for the very best defense to prevent him from accomplishing the pass. The essence of the forward pass is a high-class individual performance. It is extremely difficult to train a successful forward passer in one season. A coach and team are extremely fortunate that find among the players an accomplished passer. Such a man creates an effective and most dangerous weapon for the offense.

10

IX

GENERALSHIP AND QUARTERBACK PLAY

GENERAL CONSIDERATIONS

CONDUCT of Quarterback: The quarterback after every scrimmage should be the first man in position. The team should see him ready, alert, cheerful, and confident.

By the way he carries himself, he can communicate to the team the kind of game he wishes them to play. If he moves briskly and calls off his signals in a snappy manner, the team will immediately follow this lead. If he is deliberate and cautious, the team will respond likewise. The carriage of the quarterback, as the team approaches the goal line, is particularly important. He should then, by leading and example, inspire carefulness and determination.

The play is often greatly affected by his manner of giving the signals. The quarterback should practice changing the character of play by voice tones. This is very important as the team approaches the goal.

The quarterback is the field captain; he is the leader of the play and, therefore, should be an experienced player, if possible. The coach should not hesitate to take an experienced man from any position on the team and put him at quarterback, if it is practicable. It is not a good plan to have a man other than quarterback give the signals.

The moment the ball is down, the center should be over it ready for the next play, with the quarterback behind him, always showing himself to the team as alive, sure of himself, aggressive. He must be skilled in making quick decisions. He must remember that, when there are two or three things that can be done, it is best to do one of them confidently and without a moment's delay, even though it be the second-best choice, rather than delay and shake the team's confidence in his judgment.

Preliminary to the direction of the play in the games, the quarterback should know as far as possible the weight, age, and experience of every member of the opposing team. In fact, it is often a good plan to throw your

spare plays at the youngest and most inexperienced man on the opposing side. By
careful study of the newspapers a quarterback can often familiarize himself with many
of the weaknesses of players and of teams.
His knowledge concerning his own men and
team should, of course, be infinitely greater.
He should have his plays listed, and this
list should be revised from time to time,
eliminating from the top of the column the
weaker plays. At the end of the year some
quarterbacks have put on a small card a
short list of powerful plays, combinations,
and methods which they memorized beyond
the point of overlooking, even in the struggle
of a game. Some quarterbacks have carried
such a card into games with them to consult
when in the back field.

Basic Principles in Choice of Plays

There are certain basic principles in the
choice of plays by a quarterback which, long
experience has shown, a quarterback can vio-
late only under the most exceptional circumstances. All good generalship rests upon
these basic principles. The work of any particular quarterback who has been unusually
successful will be found either consciously or

unconsciously to rest upon these principles. They are rarely violated with impunity.

The first of these great principles is, *An advance by rushing of more than 40 yards is rarely successful.* Experience has shown that the great concentration and stress of the rushing attack can be maintained, without break, against strong opposition for a distance of not more than 40 yards. This rule, of course, does not apply where the opponent is weak and the distance can be gained in two or three plays. The rule applies to an advance through stout resistance, where the going is hard and rough. Experience has shown that if an attack against a defense of this nature is persisted in over a stretch of ground for more than 40 yards, fumbles will result, due to a break in the offense, or there will be a tie-up in the play, or the defense will have sized up the attack successfully. A quarterback adhering to this principle should plan to use his rushing attack over stretches of not more than 40 yards. It must be borne in mind, however, that this rule may be modified to a certain extent, where a long run or an unusual gain is sifted in during the rushing advance.

The second great rule of generalship is,

Never lose the ball on downs. The value of the ball to a football team is measured in yards by the distance the team is able to kick it. We may say that, in general, the ball is worth 35 yards. It is apparent that if we surrender the ball on downs in any part of the field, we simply hand the defensive team 35 yards. No such policy can be pursued with success. It is vital that a quarterback realize the supreme necessity of never failing to kick the ball forward when the attack is stopped.

This rule is subject to a certain modification when the attack is close to the opponent's goal. Here the quarterback should either kick into the corner, shoot a drop kick for the goal, or play a scoring pass. All three of these methods are offensive moves, and the particular one to be chosen depends upon the distance the ball is from the opposing goal and the particular situation at the time.

The third basic principle of generalship, which, in a way, is a corollary of the preceding two already stated, is, *Press the kicking game.* We know from a great many years' experience in football that it is impossible to rush the ball over half the length of the field. We know through our experience with the modern game that it is impossible to pass the

ALONZO A. STAGG,
UNIVERSITY OF
CHICAGO

COLONEL
ERNEST GRAVES,
ARMY

FIELDING H. ("HURRY UP") YOST,
UNIVERSITY OF MICHIGAN

PERCY D. HAUGHTON,
HARVARD UNIVERSITY

WALTER CAMP "FATHER OF AMERICAN FOOTBALL" (Inset Pictu

ball up and down the field against a good defense. We know that the mixture of passing with rushing offers a good defense an excellent opportunity to deprive the offensive team of the ball in midfield or in the attacking team's territory. The only sound rule for advancing the ball down the field against an equal opponent is either to outkick the opponent or to gain more territory by a combinaton of rushing and kicking. If the defending team can kick as far as the offensive team, it is apparent that the superior yardage can be obtained by a certain amount of rushing— say twenty yards or so—followed by a good kick. If the offense can outkick the opponents by reason of a better kicker or a favorable wind, the proposition is, of course, exceedingly simple. The problem is stated in one phrase—*Press the kicking game.* Many coaches are never satisfied with their material unless they can find among the players a first-class kicker. Such a player is a tremendous asset to any team because he really is the main feature of the attack.

The fourth great principle of generalship is, *Make and play for the breaks.* The problem of defeating a weaker team is simple. But the problem of defeating an equal or better team generally turns on the application of this rule, and this application, in turn, depends upon a particular team and situation. For instance, a close study of the opponent may show that its weakness lies in defending against the forward pass, or catching kicks, or defending the passer or kicker, or in a particularly poor player. In most of these instances the quarterback can guide the play, so as to take advantage of these weaknesses of the opponent. In other words, he should *play to the opponent's weaknesses*. This is one of the great basic principles of generalship, which not only applies to the work of the quarterback on the field, but is a guiding rule for the coach in determining matters of policy while developing the team for a particularly hard contest.

Certain basic principles have been enunciated above. Herewith are stated certain general rules for the choice of particular plays in any contest. These rules and the basic principles already laid down have been the basis of most of the successful quarterback play in the game of football. Long experience has shown that they can be violated only with great peril to the perhaps reckless quarterback and the team under his command. It will pay all quarterbacks to study and meditate with great care concerning these principles and rules.

1. No rule is absolute; break any rule in order to succeed.
2. Never lose the ball on downs—that is, get its full value forward by kicking or by a scoring play.
3. In your territory:
   (a) If outkicking opponents, go to position and kick. *Press kicking game.* Exception: at times, ball may be rushed to steady team or when in danger of kicking to fair catch.
   (b) If outkicked, hold the ball as long as possible, playing slowly and carefully for the period.
4. In opponent's territory, hold ball as long as possible, ending with scoring play if possible.
5. In general watch for:
   (1) Spreading in opponent's line.
   (2) Boxing the tackle.
   (3) Open space in back field.
   (4) Critical positions.
6. Convinced that the game is an even break, take a chance outside your 40-yard line.
7. Fake kick when kicker is hurried at dangerous opponent.
8. Inside your 20-yard line do not hold on to ball too long. *No wide runs.*
9. Take chances, provided there is nothing to lose.

Quarterback Drills

Only a very few coaches know how to train a quarterback. The following drills will prove an excellent guide for obtaining a standard performance from quarterbacks:

(a) Voice and Bearing Drill.

In this drill, a team or skeleton team is assembled either from substitutes or quarterbacks, and the quarterback candidates are required to call formations and signals. He should shift the team and change his field position slightly between each play. The coach, by example or by criticism, shows the quarterback the actual technique of assuming his position, the manner of giving his signals, and the method of switching his formations. The quarterback should be taught the paramount importance of the use of his voice. He is like an officer in command of troops, and he must be able to get his command across in the proper manner. A good voice is an exceedingly desirable asset. In this drill, the quality of the voice tones should be brought out. A clever quarterback can produce determined concentrated play by inserting that quality into his voice. He

can also produce fire and dash from certain
matters of command. Unhappily, he can,
by an unfortunate use of his voice, also bring
about nervousness and start his men before
the ball is in play. This drill may be practiced with only three men—all quarterbacks.
One candidate should play the quarterback
position, the other two candidates playing
the positions of center and halfback, re-
spectively.

(b) FIELD POSITIONS.

After the quarterback candidates have
mastered the technique of handling the ball
and have acquired the proper bearing and tone
of voice, they should be given drills in field
positions. The group outlined above should
be moved from position to position on the
field of play—the coach calling a hypothetical
down and distance, the quarterback calling
the formation and signal for the play. Discussion of critical situations and positions is,
of course, an exceedingly interesting part of
this drill. The quarterback group should be
taken to the following critical positions:
(1) The ball two yards in front of either of
his own goal posts. (2) The ball within a
yard of the goal line and two yards from any

corner. (3) The ball two yards from either
side line. (4) The ball six yards from either
side line. (5) The ball on the opponent's 4-
yard line, etc. The coach, in each of
these particular situations, calls the down and
distance, and may, in addition, prescribe
such other conditions as may make the situation critical, as, for instance, the ball on the
opponent's 10-yard line in front of the goal
posts, third down, ten to go, five seconds to
play, score 7 to 6 against you.

(c) WATCHING FOR SPREADS AND OPEN
SPACES.

The third quarterback drill is handled as
follows: Two complete teams, either first and
second, or, if more convenient, third and
fourth, are assembled. The quarterback is
required to shift the formations back and
forth, open and close them, and call the signal
for the most advantageous play resulting
from defensive players being out of position.
The coach should require the defensive players to take improper distances and intervals
in order to develop the quarterback. For
instance, a guard at times should leave an
excessive gap between himself and the center
or tackle, or a wing back should move up

close to the rush line. The quarterback
should be required to call the answering play
immediately. After the quarterback has developed a few days under this training, he
should be required, by shifting the formation
and by close analysis of the defense, to pick
flaws where he can find them. An experienced
quarterback will rise a step higher and, in
shifting or assuming a formation, call a particular play and get it off with a surprise
element added to it. This is particularly
applicable to the forward pass. A good
quarterback can line up his team and throw
the pass often before the defense is ready
for it.

(d) SCORING.

It has been said of quarterbacks that all
that is required of them is to catch kicks and
to score. They should have daily drill at
both requirements. Scoring drill is handled
by requiring the quarterback to take positions in the opponent's territory while at
either group or individual drill, and then to
call the proper plays for scoring. The coach
may call the down and distance. After the
quarterback has developed, however, he will
make his own decisions. Whenever he is

drilling in opponent's territory he should
train the team in the execution of the critical
plays upon which he proposes to rely for
scoring. For instance, he may drill the attack in driving over for a score when on the
opponent's 2-yard line; or in making a
scoring pass from drop-kick formation; or
in making a wide run from drop-kick formation when the drop kick is assumed to be too
difficult.

(e) PENCIL-AND-PAPER WORK.

Quarterbacks should be worked during the
beginning of the year at night off the field
of play with a blackboard or pencil and
paper. The coach should draw a miniature
field of play, locate the ball thereon, assume
the down and distance, and require the
quarterback to call the formation and signal.
In this manner the quarterback can be
trained in the idea of watching for spreads,
open spaces, players out of position, etc.

The above drills are not complicated
nor do they require a great deal of time.
They should be so handled that the drills will
occupy only that period allotted to group
work in the early part of the season. Con-

siderable stress should be laid upon getting the quarterback in condition to handle his attack at the very beginning of the season.

OVERCOACHING

Great care should be exercised to avoid overcoaching. At every stage of the game the quarterback should be encouraged to make his own decisions. Everything possible should be done to develop his initiative and confidence. After the season is two or three weeks old the quarterback coach should retire to a position of friendly criticism and encouragement. In this manner only can the quarterback be trained in self-reliance and daring.

Following is the general theory of the use of the various methods of attack:

THE KICKING GAME

The kicking game should be resorted to only when one's kicker is superior to that of the opponents. The ideal kick is to send the ball down the field and toward the side line, so that, when the opposing team lines up, its players will be "boxed" against the side line and be compelled to kick the ball to the center of the field or to resort to a long end run in that direction. The double advantage of kicking the ball to the opponent's side line is obvious: the kicker has in all probability gained from 30 to 40 yards on his kick; the opposing kicker is obliged to kick and thereby lose the ball to the other side somewhere in the center of the field. Of course, if the opposing kicker can kick directly over the center and down the side line, he can thereby place the other team at a disadvantage on the side line. But, unless he is an unusually reliable kicker, he will kick toward the center of the field and run the risk of one of the opposing players running the ball back.

However, the successful prosecution of the kicking game is not dependent upon this rather theoretical kicking from the center to the side and the reverse. On the contrary, generally all that can be expected of the kicker is to get off a good kick straight down field. A good kick straight ahead is quite sufficient. But where the kicker is unusually skillful he can often apply the above theoretical rule with great success.

When the team is kicking within 40 or 45 yards of the opponent's goal, the kick should be directed outside at the 5-yard or 10-yard line, compelling the opponents to kick out to a fair catch.

Should a team be kicking from behind its own goal line, it should kick into the side belt invariably, keeping the opposing team from a fair catch.

On a very windy day it is often desirable to try an extremely high kick, even though a short one, in order to try the nerve of the opposing back field and to develop a muff.

The quick kick is strong when there is a kicker capable of getting his distance in that manner. It quite often gets the ends and tackles down the field unblocked, and it has the element of surprise.

In the last minutes of a half, high short kicks are a good means of trying for a fluke score.

Just as the kicking game is played with the superior kicker, so *the rushing game* is played by a team of superior power. Though a team is better grounded in the finer points of the game, a more powerful opponent can often change the complexion of the game by refusing to kick the ball and by hammering the opposing team in all parts of the field.

The rushing game consists in going for the

11

10-yards' distance repeatedly. No rules can be given for the selection of the plays, because they vary with the team, the opponents, and the game. But the following underlying principle may be established: Given one weak point on the opposing line, there is, theoretically, the possibility of a steady advance, since in order to strengthen that point some other point must be weakened. The quarterback, by watching the feet and the heads and shoulders of the opposing players, can tell what point has been weakened. Thus with one weak point there can be a kind of pendulum advance, first striking the weak point, and then, when that is re-enforced, striking the point from which re-enforcement has been drawn.

It should be noticed that in the rushing game the opposing line will play wide in the center of the field and close in as you approach their goal line, so that advance may be made from tackle to tackle when between the 25-yard lines, whereas within 25 yards of the goal line the quarterback must watch carefully for the closing in of the opposing line and hold himself ready to roll a play around the tackle rather than smash through the line.

To test the rushing game, try the plays that have proved strongest in practice. If they go, save them for scoring distance.

As you approach the score, stick to the plays that have been going; don't try new plays on the goal line.

Do not allow yourself to play the entire game in the side belt; it cuts off half of your plays. Either rush the ball outside and take it in 15 yards, or sacrifice a play for position and, by a long end run, take the ball into the center of the field.

In general, you cannot carry the ball more than 40 yards.

There is a combination of kicking and rushing which can be played against a team having a superior kicker. Theoretically, this is played by making up the distance lost, due to the failure of the kicking game, by superiority in the rushing game. The team, on receiving the ball from a kicker, must carry it back the distance gained by the opponents in kicking, and a little more, too.

The combination game is the one ordinarily played, even when you have a superior kicker, because rushing the ball gives confidence to your own team and teaches your opponents your power; while the kicking game, to a certain extent, gives your opponents a rest. It must be remembered that the ball cannot be carried by rushing more than 40 yards, except under exceptional conditions. When extended beyond 40 yards, the probability of a fumble is so great that it is exceedingly dangerous to persist in holding on to the ball. This rule may be violated in the very beginning of the game, when the opponents are off their feet; at the very end of the game, when either you or your opponents are trying desperately for a score; or on a windy day when scoring distance is considerably increased.

The forward pass, as an element in the attack, is used in combination with the kicking and rushing offense. The quarterback, foreseeing that the rushing attack is stopped, may pass in any position outside his 40-yard line. Should he pass when well out from the opponent's goal, he should choose that character of pass which will not be intercepted. Should he pass close to the opponent's goal, he should attempt a scoring pass. The forward pass is an extremely strong, critical play, particularly for scoring. It is doubly strengthened when the element of surprise is present. A team that is unusually skillful in passing can often play a combination rushing and passing game with great success.

Technique of Handling the Ball

The following statement of quarterback technique applies only where the ball passes through a quarterback playing up under the line:

The first requisite of a play is that the ball shall be safely lodged in the hands of the runner. The play of the center and the quarterback is subordinate to this necessity. The quarterback and the center should study each other's play. The center should make any changes the quarterback desires, in order that the ball may be more safely or easily handled. The center's play is always subordinate to a safe pass to the quarterback. Putting out the opponent, making a hole, or any other detail of his play must not be considered as important as passing the ball safely to the quarterback.

In receiving the ball, the quarterback has, with his hands and arms and body, what may be called three cups. These cups are formed: first, by the hands; second, by the forearms; and third, by the arms and the body. The ball, when tossed by the center to the quarterback, will pass from the ground to the ground in a small arc. The long axis of the ball is always horizontal. The top of this arc is the point at which the ball is received by the hands of the quarterback. At this point the ball has neither an upward nor a downward motion. If the quarterback receives the ball before it reaches the top of its arc, the upward motion of the ball strikes the hands, producing what is known as fighting the ball—that is, the ball rebounds from the hands. If the hands are moved forward while the ball is moving toward them, fighting the ball also results. It is one of the common causes of fumbles. Hard passing also causes rebounds.

Should the hands be below the top of the arc, the quarterback loses valuable time, because he allows the ball to rise and then to begin to fall. The ball should be received at the top of the arc, and, if it is necessary to quicken the time, it should be done by making the arc smaller or by tending to receive the ball while it is rising. The hands

of the quarterback should not be thrust out
to receive the ball at the last moment. They
should always be in position at the top of the
arc ready for the ball and a second or two
before the ball is put in play. The hands
are held like a small cup, palms up, fingers
extended and wide apart, the little fingers
adjacent and separated by about five or six
inches. The palms of both hands are under
the path of the flight of the ball. The ball
rises and the hands receive and draw it in.

Receiving the ball in the second cup is
brought about by the ball rolling over the
hands into the forearms and touching the
upper arm. When the first cup fails the
second and third are rendered certain by
closing in the elbows and knees. Should the
first two cups fail and the ball roll between
the arms, it should lodge in the pit of the
stomach and be surrounded by both arms
and thighs. A quarterback should always
try to use the first cup, no matter what the
conditions are. Sometimes it is impossible
to handle a wet, muddy, and slimy ball
with your hands alone. A quarterback will
then find himself using the second and third
cups.

The general position of the quarter is as

follows: Face the center, one foot advanced
five or six inches beyond the other, knees bent
as desired, body bent at the waist, hands and
arms held well forward. This permits you to
turn with equal facility to either side. The
quarterback should, however, vary his feet
with the play, putting forward either foot as
desired. The only rule that he must never
break is that which forbids his disclosing the
play to the opposing team. He may work at
times even with one knee on the ground.

The quarterback, receiving the ball from
the center, draws his hands back with the
flight of the ball toward the side of the body
to which he is to pass, fixes the ball in his
hands for the pass, at the same time turning
his body at the waist, turning his head, and
turning his eyes on to the runner. He is, at
the same time, adjusting his feet into any
position he may consider desirable to facil-
itate the pass.

There are, in general, three passes: the
pass for close plays from tackle to tackle, the
pass for plays outside tackle, and the pass
for end plays. The most important is the
pass for plays from tackle to tackle. The
essential that governs the play of the quarterback on this pass is that he shall not interfere

with the runner or the play. In order not to do so and at the same time make a safe and sure pass, he is obliged to swing up under the line, keeping out of the path of the play. Otherwise, he will either strike the runner and throw him out of his path or, by getting slightly in his way, cause the runner to sheer off out of the path. As the runner approaches, the quarterback must be able to place the ball in the runner's body and then withdraw, leaving the runner a free path.

The pass for plays outside of tackle is a short, quick float, whereas for an end run the pass is made on the run to the back, after both are well started. In the latter case the pass is an easy float.

When a play has failed, the quarterback should know exactly what caused it to fail. He should know which men were in their proper places, and which were not. Often it is impossible for a quarterback to watch this and go into a play at the same time. But there are quarterbacks who can do both. However, a quarterback should be compelled to give his first attention to the direction and supervision of the offense.

A valuable exercise for the quarterback is to receive the ball from the center and then swing up under the line, practicing passes. As the center passes the ball, he should move forward. During the first half of the year the center and quarter should do this daily, and they should return to this exercise whenever there is a tendency to fumble.

The quarterback should know every back on the squad. He should make it a point to get some practice with all of them, and regular practice with the regular backs. He should learn every detail of the pass desired by each back, and endeavor to conform to that as far as practicable.

Backs often object greatly to the stand of the quarter, on the ground that his legs interfere with the view of the ball. The quarter must rectify this by continued practice with the individual backs. The fact that the back does not see the ball in any play is no excuse for any failure on his part. The back must know the quarterback and the center so well that he can tell when the ball goes in play, whether he sees it or not. Throughout the year quarterbacks and the other backs must practice constantly to perfect the passing and receiving. Of course, the position of the quarterback cannot be arbitrarily assigned for the benefit of the backs. Both must yield a little to the other's wishes.

Conclusion

The writer is well aware that many football teams use methods of play different from those he has outlined, but the history of success in football shows that the best teams have played largely in accordance with these methods. The most successful teams have been built along these lines.

Whether the direct pass or the indirect pass is used is of no consequence in so far as the principles of generalship apply. In most cases success has followed the system of generalship outlined herewith.

THE END